I Want My Daddy

BY THE SAME AUTHOR

CASEY WATSON

THE *SUNDAY TIMES* BESTSELLING AUTHOR

I Want My Daddy

Scared and alone, little Ethan just needs to be loved

HARPER
element

This book is a work of non-fiction based on the author's experiences. In order to protect privacy, names, identifying characteristics, dialogue and details have been changed or reconstructed.

HarperElement
An imprint of HarperCollins*Publishers*
1 London Bridge Street
London SE1 9GF

www.harpercollins.co.uk

HarperCollins*Publishers*
Macken House, 39/40 Mayor Street Upper
Dublin 1, D01 C9W8, Ireland

First published by HarperElement 2023

3 5 7 9 10 8 6 4

A catalogue record of this book is
available from the British Library

PB ISBN 978-0-00-848491-0
EB ISBN 978-0-00-848492-7

Printed and bound in the UK using 100%
renewable electricity at CPI Group (UK) Ltd

Dedication

I'd like to dedicate this story to all of those foster carers who continue to do what they do best. In spite of all the pitfalls, the lack of funding and the failure of local authorities who refuse to acknowledge foster carers as paid employees with the same rights as other workers, you still roll up your sleeves and get on with it. You are honestly saving lives, providing love and understanding where there is often none, and giving these children a chance at normality. I admire and respect every single one of you, and I know it's challenging and at times it's heart-breaking, but keep soldiering on, you are amazing!

Acknowledgements

As always, I need to offer some heartfelt thanks. To my fabulous agent, Andrew Lownie, and the incredible team at HarperCollins – my publishing family, whose skill and expertise continue to bring these stories to you so brilliantly.

I must also give thanks to my friend and partner-in-writing-crime, Lynne Barrett-Lee. We've become such a team now that we can almost finish one another's sentences. And often do … When we're not busy writing, that is.

Once again, I cannot pass up the opportunity to thank my amazing family and friends, who continue to keep me sane, and support me in myriad ways. I simply could not do what I do without you.

Finally, I'd like to acknowledge you, my lovely readers. Reading your reviews is all the encouragement I need to keep sharing stories of these so often forgotten children. You are the best. I send my love to you all.

Chapter 1

When I first felt the sensation of a sudden weight on my body, I was deep into a dream about my upcoming birthday. A huge cake had been wheeled towards me and (this being a dream, of course) somehow I knew exactly what was coming next. At any moment, I'd hear a bang and Tyler would pop out of the centre, accompanied by hundreds of party poppers and streamers, and with icing all over his face. But still the weight pressed across my back, as if determined to try and wake me, and when the sound came it wasn't the celebratory fanfare I'd expected. No – something suspiciously like the ringtone of my mobile phone.

'Casey!' Mike hissed, removing his arm as I rolled over. 'I can't reach your bloody phone! Can't you *hear* it?'

The dream vaporised, replaced by the shadowy shapes of our still-unfamiliar bedroom. I reached across to the bedside table and patted around until my hand finally rested on the vibrating phone. Squinting at the time on it, I realised it was 3.20 a.m. I sat bolt upright, in an instant feeling very much awake; a call at this hour obviously had to be important.

And almost certainly not in a good way. 'Hello,' I said, trying to sound calm, even though I was immediately filled with dread. (I think almost everyone would recognise the feeling. When you have grown-up children, grandchildren and elderly parents, a phone call in the early hours can never mean anything good.)

'Sandra Robinson,' a crisp female voice said. 'EDT.'

EDT. Short for the Emergency Duty Team with Social Services. So, definitely some poor soul was in trouble, and in need, but I could breathe again because my own family were, at least, okay.

'I'm so sorry to ring you at this ungodly hour,' Sandra went on, 'but we need an urgent placement for a child, Mrs Watson. As in, I have to tell you, right now. I have the police on another line waiting for a decision and a destination. It's a five-year-old little boy – his name is Ethan – and once I've given the go-ahead to the police I can tell you what we know. Is this something you could help with? I mean, you were top of the duty list anyway, hence the call. But believe me,' she added, 'it's a very short list.'

I did believe her. Year on year, it seemed to me that, while the need for foster carers was ever greater, the pool of them was getting ever smaller. Which meant that the ones still left standing had to pick up the slack in emergencies out of hours that much more often. Usually, around 30 per cent of foster carers would agree to go on the duty list at weekends and key times, but, although there were no national figures at present, it was thought that only 10 per cent were now stepping forward.

Including us. 'Give me a few moments while I speak with my husband,' I told Sandra. 'Just one minute, okay?'

Though I knew I didn't really need a minute. Mike had overheard the conversation anyway, and immediately, if blearily, nodded his consent. 'Tell her yes,' he said, sitting up, 'so they can get on their way with him, but try to find out as much as you can from them, won't you? Be good to have at least some idea of what we're dealing with.'

Which could be anything obviously – there were many possible scenarios. From a road accident to a murder, and everything in between. One thing was for sure, though. It would be something serious. No child was ever taken into care this way lightly, especially in the middle of the night. So I did exactly that, but even as I waited on the line for Sandra to come back and give me all the information she had subsequently promised, I knew that in reality she would probably know very little about the case. She wouldn't know, for example, how long the child might need to stay with us. She wouldn't know anything about his background unless he was already in the system, and she wouldn't know anything at all about his likes and dislikes, or what he was capable of, or needed, both emotionally and physically.

'There's not a lot, to be honest,' Sandra confessed, when she got back to me, having given the police our details and confirmed they could set off to our address. Our *new* address. I was still at the stage of trying to memorise the postcode. 'I don't know the child at all, because he doesn't seem to be in the system. As I said before though, he's called Ethan, Ethan Baines, and he's just gone five. I got a call half an hour ago from the police to ask if we could place him urgently. It's such a tragedy.'

She went on to tell me all she knew, and it was indeed a tragedy. Ethan, it transpired, had woken in the night to go to the toilet, and had come across his mother, collapsed on the bathroom floor. Unable to wake her, he'd become hysterical and eventually ran to the next-door neighbours, who woke up to hear his screams coming through their letter box. The man next door had gone back with him and, having seen the state of Ethan's young mother, had called emergency services – both the police and an ambulance.

'She was confirmed dead at the scene,' Sandra went on. 'Suspected heroin overdose. And as mum and boy hadn't lived in the area very long, the neighbour was unable to provide details of any extended family who could step in. In fact, he was fairly sure there was no family to speak of. No partner that he knew of, and no grandparents either. He described mum as very much a loner. And as he has a police record himself, he was unable to provide Ethan a bed for the night, even though he did offer, so the police had no alternative but to take Ethan to the station with them and contact social services.'

'Oh, the poor mite,' I said. 'That's just awful.'

'I know,' Sandra agreed. 'Apparently the poor boy is in shock now. No longer hysterical or crying – in fact, the police said he's refusing to speak at all. Has just clammed up and has been sat staring into the middle distance.'

'I'm not surprised,' I said, feeling so sad for the little boy. 'At five, he won't be able to process any of what has happened yet, I'm sure. But, oh God, when it sinks in!' I was hit then by the enormity of the situation, and tried to flip back in the filing cabinet of my mind to recall if I'd dealt with anything like this in the past. I hadn't, not really. I mean, I'd had children in the past who had lost parents, but we'd never taken in a child in the immediate aftermath like this. Because how often did it happen that a child lost a parent and there was no known relative anywhere who could be called on to help? That fact felt like another tragedy in itself.

Sandra ended the call by assuring me that someone would call me at 9 a.m. to follow everything up, and then wished me good luck. Which I knew I would need. Despite all the years I'd spent around distressed, vulnerable children, I felt suddenly, and profoundly, ill-equipped. But perhaps anyone would at half three in the morning. It just felt so bleak a thing to contemplate.

'Come on then,' Mike said, throwing the duvet off. 'I think we need coffee, love, don't you?'

'You have work in a few hours, love,' I reminded him. 'Don't you want to try and get another couple of hours' sleep and leave me to deal with this for now?'

He shook his head and stood up. 'No way will I get back to sleep now,' he said, grabbing his dressing gown from the hook on the back of the bedroom door. 'I'll go down and start the coffee. Why don't you go check the back bedroom, and make sure it's all ready for him?'

I reached for my own dressing gown and while Mike padded off down the stairs, I went across the landing and did as he suggested. Standing in the doorway, I felt a mixture of emotions. Satisfaction, that I'd only recently redecorated this room, painting it a lovely shade of yellow, then brightening it up further with splashes of reds, blues and oranges in the form of duvet covers, cushions, shelves and lighting. It was the first of many transformations we'd be embarking on, as time and budget dictated, but this one had been the priority, obviously, so we'd be ready for our next foster child. And I was pleased with it. It really was a happy-looking room. But alongside my pride in the room was its inevitable polar opposite: a gut feeling of sorrow, because in less than an hour I would be putting a young child to bed in here, a child whose mother had been cruelly ripped away from him, forever. A child who would be feeling the polar opposite of happy.

I smoothed the bedding, checked the radiator dial, switched on the bedside light and, with nothing more to be done bar popping on the heating once down in the hall, pulled the door closed again and went downstairs.

'I've put the heating on,' Mike said, reading my mind as he passed me a coffee. 'I wonder if he'll have any stuff with him. You'd think someone might have packed him a bag or something, yes?'

'Hopefully, love,' I said, 'because, God knows, he will need to wake up to at least *something* that's familiar to him. Poor kid. It sounds like his mum was all he had. I mean, what do we even say to him, Mike? What *do* you say? I don't want to make things any worse.'

Mike shrugged and pulled out one of the bar stools by the breakfast bar for me to sit on. 'I don't think anybody would know what to do in a situation like this, Case. I suppose we play it by ear, just follow the lad's lead. If he isn't up for talking, then we allow him to be silent. Doesn't mean we can't talk to *him*. I'm sure we can do that.'

'You're right,' I said, 'we've gone into situations blindly before and worked it out, so we can do it again. I just hate not having a plan, even a loose plan, you know?'

Mike smiled. 'I do, love, but on this occasion, that's all the plan we *can* have. We just follow the boy's lead. We make him feel safe, we put him to bed, we try to chat – small talk, that's all – and we do this on repeat until he's ready for more. Without us knowing a bit more about the circumstances, about *him*, that's really as much planning as we can do for now, isn't it?'

For all that my husband generally stayed in the background as far as the day-to-day nitty-gritty of fostering went, it was at times like this that I really appreciated his calm, matter-of-fact approach to everything. While my mind was whirring with all the potential scenarios we could be facing, Mike's wasn't second-guessing the 'what ifs' at all. He was just accepting the uncertainty and asking me to roll with it too. I immediately felt calmer; plus it wouldn't do for me to show my anxiety to a poor child who was no doubt drowning in it. I took a deep breath, gave Mike a hug, and then sat down and drank my coffee. All we could do now was wait for the familiar sounds of car doors being clunked shut and feet crunching on gravel, as yet another child was brought to us in the car of a stranger. Only this time it wouldn't be a tired social worker's equally tired jalopy; it would be a police car. A *police* car. In the dead of night, too. While his mother – from what we knew perhaps his only loving constant – would be on her final journey, to the local morgue.

Chapter 2

By the time the police car arrived, it was almost 5.00 a.m., just an hour before Mike usually got up for work yet still pitch-black outside, with no moon. I grimaced as I glanced out at the late September pre-dawn, and wondered, not for the first time, how on earth people managed to drag themselves out of bed at this godforsaken hour during the cold, dark months. A dark welcome indeed for our newest arrival, and in more ways than one, I thought, as I watched a young policewoman get out of the back seat. She then leaned in, presumably to unclip a seatbelt, before extracting a small boy who was clutching a blanket that obscured his face and then carrying him, held tightly against her chest, to our door.

'Hello, sweetheart,' I said quietly to Ethan, leaning in to try and get a glimpse of his face. This, however, only served to make him try to bury his head further into the police officer's neck. She smiled a weary smile at me. It must have been a harrowing night for her.

'Hi. Casey is it?' she asked as she stepped into the hall, then followed me into the living room where Mike was waiting. 'I'm PC Stacey Hinchcliffe,' she said, then, nodding at the form currently bundled against her, 'and this is Ethan. And hiding underneath this super-cool blanket is a toy puppy from *Paw Patrol*. His name is Chase, isn't that right, Ethan? And Chase is very, very brave, just like Ethan is trying to be.'

She then tried to prise the little child from her shoulder, which only made him cling onto her ever harder. Any port in a storm, I thought. She had become his *de facto* safe place in a stormy scary sea. 'Ethan, sorry, honey,' she whispered to him, 'I know you're very tired, but this is Casey and Mike who we told you about. You're sleeping here tonight, and I'll bet you have a lovely room ready, and a comfy bed to rest in. Can I just pop you and Chase down on the sofa for a minute in case my important radio goes off?'

The mention of the radio seemed to do it. Ethan loosened his grip and allowed her to place him gently onto the sofa, where his face immediately crumpled and he started to cry, stuffing his tiny fists into his eye sockets as he did so. It couldn't have been a more wretched thing to watch.

'I want my mummy!' he sobbed. 'Where's Mummy? I want Mummy!'

By this time, a second officer had joined us in the living room, having been held up in the patrol car, making a call. It was obvious from his expression that he'd had a long night as well, and, like the rest of us, was distressed at not being able to help the poor boy, who was sobbing harder now, beneath the blanket that was all but covering his face again. 'I want Mummy! Where's Mummy? I want *Mummy*!'

I was grateful for Mike, then, when he decided upon action.

'I tell you what, Ethan,' he said, crouching down and holding one hand out towards the child, 'bring Chase and your blanket, and let's you and I go take a look for a nice bed for you to snuggle into. Then, after you've had a good long sleep, and it's morning, we can make some phone calls and find out all we can about your mummy. Okay?'

The sobbing abated slightly, and Ethan peeked out from beneath his blanket and stared at Mike through a mess of dirt and tears. He took a huge, stuttering breath then, as if making a decision, nodded. 'Okay,' he said brokenly, 'but just for twenty minutes.'

Mike nodded too, as if this was the most natural request in the world. 'Twenty minutes it is, then, kiddo. Come on then,' he added, as Ethan, to my surprise, took his hand. Then, without another word from either, Mike led the still-whimpering little boy from the room, while I filed that very precise 'twenty minutes' into my brain.

The moment they'd left the room, PC Hinchcliffe's shoulders visibly sagged. She sighed heavily. 'So bloody *sad*,' she said, with considerable feeling. 'I haven't had a clue what to say to him. No idea. It's been *horrendous*.' She shook her head then. 'Though I'm not sure your husband should have given him hope about his mother,' she added anxiously. 'A social worker has already been clear with him that she's died.'

I felt sorry for her. She didn't look to be much more than in her mid-twenties. I didn't doubt she'd seen some grim things during her time with the police, but perhaps this was a first. Whether that was true or not, I didn't know, obviously, but it was clear the whole experience had shaken her. 'Yes, well, he's only five,' I pointed out gently, 'and he doesn't understand that at all right now. No matter how clearly it's been spelled out, it's absolutely unimaginable for him to have to think he will never see his mummy again at the moment. Yes, *we* know he won't, but it's going to take some time before Ethan can even begin to acknowledge or understand that fact, let alone start the process of coming to terms with it.'

PC Hinchcliffe sighed again. 'Yes, I suppose. I guess you know what you're doing. I just feel so sorry for the little mite. It's just awful, isn't it? Anyway, are you going to be alright if we leave now?' she asked, glancing at the other officer, who was scrolling through some notes. He looked over and smiled grimly at me.

'Unless you've any questions?' he added. 'I believe a social worker will be bringing out all the necessary paperwork later on this morning, but, officially, our shift finished at 2.00 a.m., and I think we both need to go home. And for my part, I need a cuddle off my kids, frankly.'

I knew exactly what he meant. 'Oh, my goodness, of *course* you must go,' I told them. 'We will be fine, honestly. We've dealt with bereavement before. Never like this, and never so suddenly, to be honest, but we'll find our way, don't worry. You get off home.'

I let the exhausted officers out and locked the front door behind them. It was growing light now. A new day. The birds had started singing to welcome it. The first day of that poor little lad's radically changed life. I hovered for a few moments at the bottom of the stairs. All was quiet. Should I go up and join Mike and Ethan? Perhaps not. Quiet was good. Sleep would be the poor child's only respite. No sense potentially disturbing him if he was settled. I headed instead for the kitchen. Tired as I was, there was no way I could sleep again now so, nothing for it, more coffee.

I'd just plucked the kettle from its stand when Mike came in and joined me. He looked upset and gaunt. 'He's asleep,' he confirmed quietly. 'Practically as soon as he lay down – fully clothed and everything. I managed to get his trainers off but other than that I left him as he was. Seemed silly to try and change him into jim-jams.'

'That's fine, love,' I said. 'Did he say anything at all?'

Mike shook his head. 'No, not really. I just lay him down and told him not to worry, that he should sleep and we could talk when he woke up, and that was it. A couple of mumblings, but he was out like a light.' Mike pushed his hands through his hair. He'd obviously been dwelling on what he'd said to the little boy. 'I hope I did right,' he said. 'You know, telling him not to worry. It just seemed crazy to say anything else to him, state he was in. I know sleep won't change things, but at least he's getting rest now …'

I went across and hugged him. 'You did absolutely the right thing, love. There'd be no way he could take it in yet. Might not for days, or even weeks. Better to let the dust settle. Get some more info on what happened. And we know nothing of his background yet, do we? All we know for sure is that he's traumatised and distressed. He won't want to be here – he's been dragged away from everything he knows and he's going to be angry about it when he realises he can't go home. All we can do is play it by ear, take each moment as it comes, and hope we keep on doing the right thing. Do what you said to do, basically.'

Even as I said it, I knew it wouldn't be that simple. Everything we did from here on in would have a huge impact on Ethan, one way or another, and the next few days were going to be so, so important. In my sleep-deprived state, the task ahead for us suddenly felt monumental. The rest of this child's life would be affected by what happened next. I usually felt that no part of my job was insurmountable, but for some reason the immediate future with this child felt very scary indeed. Perhaps it was just the hour. We all feel more vulnerable at night, I reasoned, especially after such a harrowing awakening. I thought of what the male police officer had said, and I wished I could have a cuddle off my kids as well. But in the meantime, Ethan was at least soundly sleeping. Which would give us precious time to emotionally regroup, so we were in the right place to best help him when he did wake up.

Mike, meanwhile, had to go to work. So, while he went up to shower and dress, I took my coffee into the living-room area, turning the TV on so it could drone away to itself in the background while I pondered – as I couldn't help – to the way life could turn on a sixpence. And so cruelly. And for any of us, at any moment. Our illusion of having control over our lives was just that.

I felt helpless and nervous about how to act when the boy finally woke. The questions and demands would start again for sure, and I willed the time forward to when offices would open and social workers would pick up their messages. Fingers crossed I'd be among the first of their morning calls. I was most of the time happy to go in blind and muddle through. But I needed help with this one, and I didn't mind admitting it.

Chapter 3

I realised, to my shame, that I must have drifted off on the sofa, because for the second time that morning I was woken by the sound of my ringing mobile. The sound was distant, though, because it was still on its charger on the kitchen worktop and I was far away – well, to my mind – in the 'living room' bit of our cavernous new open-plan downstairs.

I scrabbled to my feet, picking up the remote as I did so; the telly was still chuntering away to itself and I could see from the screen that it was almost 9 a.m. How had *that* happened? I couldn't recall the last time I'd fallen asleep on the sofa – on *any* sofa, for that matter. I was too fond of my bed. And never needed an excuse to head up to it.

Grabbing my phone from the kitchen counter, I saw it was Christine, my lovely supervising social worker. Relief rushed through me but, alongside it, guilt.

'Oh, Christine, can you give me just a second?' I asked her. 'Sorry – I've only just woken up and I'm in a kerfuffle. I just need to go up check Ethan's still sleeping.'

'No problem,' she said. 'I'll hang on the line and drink my cuppa. Take your time. It's a big mug. You head off.'

I did as she instructed, and hurried off to check on him, taking the stairs two at a time, phone still in hand, anxious now that he might have woken up, disorientated and frightened. Had he called out to me, bless him? And had I slept right through it?

Happily, I opened the door to find the room dark and silent – well, almost silent; I could hear the sound of very soft, childish snores.

I tiptoed across to the bed, where his tiny form was huddled, and then retreated without doing anything that might make him stir, despite an almost irresistible urge to place a reassuring hand on his back. He looked so small and so peaceful, so blissfully unaware. It immediately brought a lump to my throat.

'It's okay,' I whispered, once I was back out on the landing. 'The poor little thing is still asleep – not that I'm surprised. He's had a hell of a night, hasn't he?'

'And you and Mike too, I imagine,' Christine answered, as I trotted back downstairs. 'D'you want to make yourself a mug of that devil's brew of yours and call me back?'

That made me smile. As my supervising social worker, Christine is my hotline to social services, the person I report to, and discuss any worries or concerns with. She replaced my former 'boss', John Fulshaw, several years ago now, and though I was anxious that anyone I was allocated hadn't a cat in hell's chance of matching up to him, I was, happily, proved very wrong. Christine's in her fifties, like me, and very warm and down to earth, and pretty much the only significant thing we have ever disagreed on is the nature of a devil's brew. Because to my mind, it's *her* drink of choice: tea.

'No worries,' I said, once I was back in the kitchen. 'I'll put you on loudspeaker and make one as we talk. And yes, it has been, and we didn't get a lot of sleep, but I'm fine. It's Mike who'll be exhausted later, bless him. He's gone to work. But the main thing is that the poor mite is safe now. He was so upset at being left with us – kept crying for his mummy – but it was obvious he was exhausted and I can't say I'm sorry; he was out like a light when Mike took him up to bed, so at least it wasn't as traumatic as it might have been.'

'Well, thank goodness for small mercies. What a terrible, terrible business. Poor little thing will be so distressed and confused. I'm guessing EDT couldn't tell you very much?' Christine continued.

'Very little. Have you been able to find out anything more yet?'

'Not a lot,' she replied. 'And to be honest, what little I've been able to amass so far isn't particularly helpful or enlightening. Brogan Baines, Ethan's mother, seems to have evaded the spotlight for a number of years so there has never been more than minimal involvement with any services. Thankfully, though, we've at least been able to make contact with her parents this morning. They're grief-stricken right now, obviously, so are unable to shed much light on any background for the moment, and I didn't want to press them just yet. You know, give them a little space. But, fingers crossed, soon we should know more.'

'Of course,' I said. 'Of course. They'll be in bits. In the meantime,' I added, crossing my actual fingers, 'does Ethan at least have a social worker? Because we urgently need some stuff for him – he came without clothes, without anything familiar, other than a blanket and one small cuddly toy. I mean, I could go through our clothes and toy boxes in the loft, but ideally he needs some of his own things around him.'

'Bless him, of course he does,' Christine agreed. 'And, no, he doesn't have anyone allocated yet. But I'm going into an urgent planning meeting in twenty – no, fifteen – minutes, and I'll make a note that you need someone out there today and that they need to pack some of Ethan's things to bring along. Will you be able to manage until this afternoon, do you think?'

'That'll be fine,' I said. 'And yes, of course. So, what little bits *do* you know? Did you manage to establish if there *are* any other family members?'

'Well, yes and no,' Christine said, going on to explain that though the hope had been that Mr and Mrs Baines, Ethan's maternal grandparents, would agree to take Ethan to live with them, this hope had already been ruled out, at least temporarily, as the couple had not seen or heard from either their daughter or their grandson in at least two years. They'd had a huge falling-out over something – Christine had yet to establish what – and had, heartbreakingly at any time but particularly given her tragic death, had no contact with their daughter or grandson since.

'Added to that,' Christine continued, 'Mr Baines has diabetes and is immobile at the moment, having recently been discharged from hospital after having his foot amputated. Mrs Baines is effectively his carer just now so they definitely can't commit to having Ethan in the immediate future. In fact, it was a flat out "no" when I spoke to them earlier. But, as I say, given how they must be feeling just now, we can forgive them for that, and hope they may have a change of heart once they've come to terms with things.'

My heart sank at this. Would they ever come to terms? And if not, did it mean this child had no one? 'What about his dad?' I tried, 'I mean, there must *be* a dad, but is he in the picture?'

'We're exploring that,' Christine said. 'The grandparents refused to say anything about him – telling in itself; makes me think they actively want him kept out of the picture – and the neighbour who called the death in had no idea who his dad might be, so it looks as though he definitely wasn't a regular visitor or anything. However, he might be known to another branch of the service – you never know – and as soon as everyone's shaken off their early morning torpor, there will be people trying to track him down, so fingers crossed.'

I sighed. I knew that even if they did track him down, this wouldn't necessarily mean that a happy ending was on the cards. If the man had had no previous contact with Ethan, there was no way social services would simply hand him over to him. And rightly so. He would be a complete stranger to him.

'So there's a lot resting on ifs, buts and good fortune then,' I mused. 'But it is what it is, I suppose. Anyway, can you phone me the minute you have a social worker assigned? At least that way I can let him know some of his things will be arriving.' Then, having mused, I asked another question. 'I don't suppose you have any advice on what to say to him when he wakes up, do you, Christine? I know it sounds feeble, but I'm terrified of making matters worse.'

'I wish,' Christine said, 'but to be honest, not really. I trust your instincts, always have. And you should too.' She then simply reiterated what both Mike and I had already said to each other; that we take direction from Ethan himself. Try to go at his pace and be honest, though not 'brutally honest', not if we could help it. Obviously try using distraction techniques if we had to, but other than that, to just be present, and loving, and nurturing.

She was right. I knew that was really all we *could* do, and that, actually, there were no right answers to my questions. Each child would react differently to grief and loss, and I was as prepared as I could be. That is, not prepared at all, if I was being honest.

After we ended the call I made a second mug of coffee and sat for a while, both hands clutched around it, looking out across the garden, through the preposterously large windows. Which weren't even windows, but a wall of what I had learned were actually called 'bifold doors'. Wall to wall, floor to ceiling, and slightly unnerving. We weren't overlooked, other than by a row of tall trees, but I couldn't help feeling exposed. Still the house was amazing; I'd never lived anywhere so modern, hence the decision – which I still couldn't believe we made so quickly – to bite our landlord's hand off when he suggested the swap. We were close to our son Kieron and his partner Lauren now, and even closer to my parents, something that was a huge weight off my mind, as I was increasingly mindful that they were elderly, and growing frailer. On top of that, like Mr Baines, my dad now had diabetes, and I was conscious that my sister Donna, who had always lived close to them, had been doing more than her fair share of supporting them.

So now that could change. And though the house move had meant Tyler's beloved bedroom was no more, I had faithfully re-created it, along with all his childhood possessions, here.

And now we had a new child. For how long, I wondered? For as long as he needed to be with us, obviously, but I sincerely hoped his grandparents could – would – step up for him. That precious connection to

23

his mother would make a world of difference to his future. *All* the difference. He'd lost his mother now, and no one could change that, but please, I thought, as I drained my mug and headed back to the staircase, *please* let him not lose his grandparents as well.

Ethan was awake when I re-entered the bedroom. His eyes were wide and watery as he looked at me, startled. He then immediately covered his face with his blanket. Just his mousey curls were visible now, brown, like his eyes.

'Morning, sweetheart,' I said softly as I crossed the room to him. 'I'm Casey. We met last night, do you remember?' I sat down on the bed just below where I could see his legs, tightly scrunched against his body. I rested a hand on his back and made gentle circular motions. 'I think it's time you and Chase came down for some breakfast. What d'you say?' Before I'd had my unintentional morning snooze, I'd made a point of Googling who Chase was, and learned all I could about him and his buddies. 'Because, you know what?' I added. 'I know all the *Paw Patrol* puppies like to eat when they wake up. So … how about I carry you downstairs?'

This seemed to do the trick, as he immediately pulled back his blanket. 'I'm a big boy,' he said, in a surprisingly firm voice. 'I don't need a carry. I need a pee, and I can do it all by myself.'

'Phew!' I said, exaggerating my relief. 'Thank goodness for that. You are *such* a big boy that I bet I couldn't carry you anyway! Come on then, I'll show you where the toilet is, shall I? And you can bring your blanket down with you. And Chase, of course.'

To which suggestion he grabbed both blanket and dog and, with an expression of what I could only describe as grim determination, he wordlessly marched to the open doorway, where he waited for me to show him where the bathroom was, hopping from one leg to the other.

It was an unlikely start to a day that turned out to be the opposite of what I'd expected. No, despite my 'be ready for anything' plan, I simply wasn't prepared for what actually transpired as the morning began to play out. There were no tears, no questions, not even a single mention of the traumatic events of the night before. Which was worrying. Because, to me, that was much more concerning a symptom than the alternative. It meant that Ethan was either emotionally wanting already, or, as a result of the trauma, actively shutting things out, and I knew from many years of experience how dangerous this was, and how adversely it could affect children for years to come.

But how to play things? Ethan was almost like an automaton, programmed simply to comply. He agreed, without hesitation, to everything I asked. Chocolate hoops for breakfast? A nod and a yes, please. Orange juice to drink? A nod and a yes, please. It was the same when I asked if he wanted to do some colouring-in, and again when I asked if he wanted to see the garden. In fact, the only thing he asked for, after about two hours of silent, solo play (his whole demeanour made it clear that he didn't want to colour *with* me), was if he could watch some TV. *Paw Patrol*, in fact, which at least didn't faze me, because I'd learned my way around a smart TV sufficiently by now that I could find my way to a whole string of episodes. So, rightly or wrongly, because my instinct was so strongly to engage with him, I left him settled on the sofa with a biscuit and more juice while I tidied around and waited for the phone to ring, suddenly so aware of how these first days and weeks could affect his mental health. I was also aware, despite so many years looking after troubled children, of how utterly clueless I felt.

I could only hope that he would be allocated an experienced social worker. One who knew how to approach helping a child who'd suffered such extreme trauma. One who would also know how to help *me* help him.

Chapter 4

Things started happening a couple of hours after I'd first spoken to Christine. An emergency planning meeting had taken place, as she'd told me would happen, and now Ethan apparently had his own social worker. I'd never heard of Lydia Heptonstall before but, according to Christine, who phoned again to give me the news, she was highly regarded within the service and, being in her fifties, like the two of us, also had decades of experience and almost certainly had seen it all. Shortly after that, Lydia herself phoned, to introduce herself to me and to say she'd be arriving at our house around lunchtime, armed with as many of Ethan's belongings as she could fit into her car.

I glanced into the living-room area from my perch at our new breakfast bar. It sounds silly, I know, but it still felt like I was on holiday, or on an Airbnb minibreak in someone else's house. I hadn't yet got used to being in my new surroundings, much less feeling as if I was at home. But it was great – and very novel – to be sitting way back in the kitchen and being able to see the whole of the downstairs living space. Well, almost all of it. As well as my open-plan kitchen, diner and lounge area, there was also another small reception room just off the hallway, for which I already had big plans. I was yet to decorate it properly, but I'd already managed to make it cosy and tasteful, imagining it would become mine and Mike's 'sanctuary'. A living space just for us, to relax in together after any children – be they grandkids or foster kids – were in bed. And since I'd filled it with the few 'posh' things we possessed – my late grandmother's crystal vases, a couple of ornaments brought back from foreign holidays and scores, literally scores, of framed family photographs – it would be a no-go area for any little ones.

But already the writing was on the wall. Because, in reality, we'd made the main living area so inviting that we'd so far hardly used our 'sanctuary' at all.

'I'll put a nice fireplace in there, with a log burner,' Mike had promised when I'd mentioned it, 'then I'm sure we'll use it for some cosy nights in the winter.'

I slipped off my stool now. We would see. I wouldn't bank on it. Not with everything else that was going on right now. Not least Kieron and Lauren's fast-approaching Christmas wedding. Besides, right now, I had other things on my mind.

'A lady called Lydia is coming to see you soon, sweetheart,' I said as I approached Ethan on the sofa. 'She's what we call a social worker and she's going to bring some of your things here. That'll be nice, won't it?'

Ethan tore his eyes away from the TV screen and looked at me suspiciously. 'What things?' he asked. 'Why's she bringing things?'

'I'm not sure what, exactly,' I said, 'but maybe some of your toys and clothes and stuff so you have some of your own belongings here.'

He shook his head. 'Me 'n' Mummy don't want no social lady at our door,' he said. 'I want the polices to come back 'n' get me and take me home.' He then added, 'Right now!' very firmly.

It was so sad to listen to and watch. This little boy clearly thought if he said his piece with anger and an air of authority I'd have to comply, but what could I say? There's no one at your home? Your mummy died?' Was it kinder to be brutally honest in cases like this? No, I decided, I wouldn't tell a lie, but I'd veer away from the words that he would definitely not want to hear just yet.

'I'm sorry, sweetheart,' I said as I started to plump some cushions. 'That's not possible right now, but hey, I've spoken to Lydia and she sounds really nice. Maybe you and she can play together with your toys when she gets here, and you can show her your Chase puppy. I'm sure she'd love to meet him.'

I continued to work my way around the living-room area as I spoke, aware that Ethan was watching my every move. 'Oh, and actually it's almost lunchtime,' I said brightly. 'I'm going to have a jam and peanut butter sandwich before she comes. What would you like to eat? Do you like jam and peanut butter sandwiches too?'

'Don't like that,' Ethan said, back to the glum monotone voice I'd heard earlier. 'I like noodles. The ones with the brown powder.'

Luckily, I knew exactly what he meant. Tyler had always gone through phases with his favourite foods. He'd become obsessed with something for months – Hobnob biscuits or bananas, to name two examples – and would eat them obsessively for a period of weeks or months. He'd gone through one a year back with BBQ beef Super Noodles, which, as ever, he ate on almost a daily basis. Then, just as suddenly as his obsession had started it had stopped, leaving me with half a cupboard full of the pesky things, as no one else would touch them. I looked upwards and gave a silent thank you to the gods of saving things 'just in case', then smiled at Ethan.

'Noodles with brown powder coming right up, then, sir,' I said, smiling at him as I gave a mock bow.

Did I see a flicker of a smile on his little face? I couldn't be positive, but I banked the knowledge that silliness on my part might at least distract this child. Exactly four minutes later – and I know this because Ethan assured me that brown powder noodles took four minutes, I placed a bowl on the breakfast bar and called him across for his lunch.

'Can you manage to climb up on that stool,' I asked, 'or shall I give you a lift?'

Ethan considered as he checked out the rather high stool, then stood there with his arms slightly held away from his body. It was a clear sign that he wanted me to pick him up, so, without saying anything, I lifted him from behind and perched him on the stool. To be honest, even I had to climb on the foot-rest thingy in order to get up on one of those things. I don't think Mike remembered I was under five foot tall when he ordered them, so Ethan was right not to attempt it.

'Mummy blows them for me,' he said once he was seated in front of his steaming bowl (I drew the line at serving them straight from the plastic pot). 'I burned my lips once and it really really hurt.'

I immediately picked up the bowl and started to simultaneously stir and blow in order to cool down the food, an action I'd performed many times with my own children, and later my grandchildren, and it got me thinking. On the surface I had no reason to believe that Ethan had been used to anything other than a caring mother. He was dressed nicely, and had been clean when he'd arrived in the early hours, and I remembered the scent of freshly washed hair on him. Yes, his speech seemed to be more in line with that of a three- or four-year-old, but he was polite enough and his vocabulary didn't seem that limited. I wondered what kind of relationship he and his mother had had.

31

In my experience it seemed as though it was often all or nothing with a drug-addicted parent. Some were that wrapped up in their habit and where their next fix was coming from that they had no time at all for their children, leaving them seriously neglected. Others, however, seemed to overcompensate. They knew that their lifestyle was completely wrong, so they went overboard with their demonstrations of affection. They would provide the most expensive toys, designer clothes, and the best food for their kids. Of course, a huge drug habit meant that those in the grip of it would have to go out shoplifting and stealing to fund their addiction, and this was usually where all the stuff came from. The reasons behind it were often complex, but for those who didn't sell everything for drugs, it was all about perception. How neighbours and schools, etc. would look at the children, and (hopefully, from the point of view of the addict) then take the view that they were indeed well cared-for, making suspicions about addiction that much less likely. Which was it here? Right now, I couldn't work out what kind of a mother Brogan Baines had been. But I supposed I'd find out soon enough.

Although Ethan couldn't climb up onto the breakfast bar stool, he could jump off it, and as soon as he'd finished his noodles, which he did, very quickly, he was down and scurried back to the sofa in front of the TV. And I realised that I would have to set some kind of routine if this placement was set to go on indefinitely.

He couldn't spend all his days watching *Paw Patrol*, that was for sure.

The sound of my mobile phone ringing cut into my thoughts, and I frowned as I saw it was the social worker, Lydia. Surely she had set off already?

She had. In fact, she was out on our street, looking for our house number, which had been an issue for everyone since we moved here. For some stupid reason, the previous tenants had put the plate with the number on below the letter box, so when our cars were on the drive, nobody could see the damn thing. It was made even worse by the fact that our next-door neighbours didn't even have a door number. So moving ours was one job Mike would have to do, for definite.

I went out to greet Lydia, and I liked her the moment I set eyes on her, just noting the way she was powering up the front path, in the kind of way that seemed to indicate she was a woman who got things done. Greying, mid-brown hair was scraped up on to the top of her head in a 'messy bun', and there was a sheen of moisture across her un-made-up face. The tell-tale signs of an age and stage of life I knew *all* about. That, teamed with comfy pumps, a pair of leggings and a parka coat all screamed out 'old school' to me, and I did like old school, especially in a social worker.

'You found us then?' I asked, laughing. 'Come on in, and here, let me grab that suitcase off you. You just get yourself in and sat down. I bet you're boiling in that coat.'

33

It was quite a large suitcase, weighty as well, and, as she was also carrying two bulging supermarket bags for life in her other hand, she was only too happy to hand it over.

'You've no idea how hot I am!' she gasped as she finally put down the bags and dragged her coat off. 'Thank God for HRT is what I say. Heaven knows what I'd be like without that.'

For some inane reason, I felt like saying, 'I hear ya, sister!' I didn't, but it was something that Kieron used to jokingly say to me before giving me a high five. I bit my tongue, however, and instead suggested, 'Tea, coffee, glass of fruit juice?'

Rather than sit down at the dining table, Lydia headed straight for the living area, where Ethan was, calling over her shoulder, 'Coffee, please, strong and black with two sugars.'

I loved this woman already! Hot and bothered as she was, she knew she had a job to do first: a child to say hello to, and hopefully put at ease before any small talk with me, the foster carer. Her heart and her priorities sat exactly where they should do, in my book, plus she was a coffee lover. Win-win. I couldn't wait to start working with this one.

A few minutes later I joined her and Ethan in the living area, armed with two mugs of coffee, and was astonished to see that Lydia was kneeling on the rug in front of the sofa, arms bent forwards, hands pointing towards Ethan, making yappy sounds. 'My highly trained paws are at your service,' she declared, causing Ethan to actually giggle.

I set the coffee down on a side table, then sat down on the footstool and just watched.

'Let's take to the sky!' Ethan shouted.

'I'm all fired up!' Lydia shouted back. At which point both she and Ethan laughed together, and I couldn't help but doff my mental cap that she knew the *Paw Patrol* lingo; this woman really was amazing.

'Oh, I have three grandchildren,' Lydia laughed when I commented on her impressive knowledge, 'and all of them are crazy about Chase and co. You know, I do believe I've watched every single episode. How about you, Ethan? Can you beat that?' she asked, turning back to him.

I had the strong impression that my presence was superfluous. 'Should I leave you for a while?' I asked.

Lydia nodded firmly. Immediately. 'If you don't mind,' she said, 'I'll have a little chat with Ethan, tell him all about my job, and then we'll have a catch-up, if that's okay.'

It wasn't a question, and was most definitely okay. If Lydia could get this reaction from him in just a few minutes, she was welcome to spend as much time with him as she wanted. I picked my mug back up and retreated back to the kitchen area, where I sat back on my stool, picked up my phone, and scrolled through my social media while I waited.

After ten minutes or so of chat, which I could only pick up intermittently, the two of them trooped upstairs and were gone for fifteen minutes, and when they came back down, Lydia showed Ethan the suitcase and the two shopping bags before settling him back down in front of the TV. A moment or two later, she finally joined me at the dining table, where I'd relocated as, being at the far end of the kitchen, it was pretty much out of Ethan's earshot.

'That was rough, actually,' she said as she pulled another chair out and sat down opposite me. 'He's using every trick in the book not to talk about his mum. Avoidance, distraction, feigned ignorance – you name it, he's doing it. I mean, he's fine talking about almost anything else, but ignores any attempt from me to speak about what happened.'

'It's quite scary, isn't it?' I said. 'He's going to need a lot of help.'

Lydia sighed. 'He is, I'm afraid, and unfortunately he will probably hate me before long, because if he's under our care for any length of time, I'm going to be seeing him quite regularly, and eventually he will have to have that conversation with me.'

'And us?' I asked. 'Are we meant to try that as well?'

Lydia shook her head, and in a way that I felt immediately reassured by. I got the strong sense that she had dealt with this kind of thing before. 'No. Not if you don't want to. I mean, it's fine if a situation arises and you can drop in the odd comment or question, but it's also fine for you to wait it out until he's ready. We are putting a support package together, a child psychologist – Ian Redfearne, he's attached to CAMHS (Children and Adolescent Mental Health Service) – and there is already a family support officer in place. It's going to be her job to pick Ethan up from you so he can continue with the visits to his dad, once we get that side of things sorted out.'

'His dad?' I asked. 'Oh, so he is definitely in the picture then? We weren't sure.'

'Oh right,' Lydia said. 'So, I imagine you won't have heard the latest on the grandparent situation either, then?'

I shook my head, and Lydia explained that Ethan's dad, Jack, was in prison at the moment and still had almost a year to serve of his sentence but, despite that, had been in the boy's life on and off, and prison visits had taken place in the past.

'So he has been known to social services then?' I asked.

'Yes, as it turns out. Apparently Dad didn't know he had a son for the first couple of years, and once he did, he secured the right to see him regularly. And going forward, fingers crossed, they will become a more regular thing,' she said. 'We feel it's important for Ethan that this relationship is built upon now, and that we work with Jack to help strengthen their bond, so that the child has a significant person in his life. The visits will be fortnightly at first and if they go well, we can up it to weekly. I've already mentioned this to Ethan and, thankfully, he is keen. He definitely wants to keep on seeing his daddy.'

'I'm not surprised,' I said, 'because even though Dad's in prison, I guess it's some form of stability for Ethan. And you mentioned the grandparents? Any change there overnight?'

It seemed yes. Lydia explained that Mrs Baines had contacted her this morning and explained that although they were grief-stricken, and their relationship with their daughter had been strained and estranged, they were now willing to undergo an assessment as potential carers for Ethan. And this despite her husband's ill health.

'So, carers then,' I said. 'They're not simply going to take him on as their grandson?'

'No, that's the thing,' Lydia said. 'They want to do it all officially, as foster carers for him, just in case a year or two down the line, Mr Baines becomes too ill to have a young lad tearing around – her words, not mine – and also the fact that under the care of social services, there will be an established support network. Might sound a bit harsh, but I guess she's being sensible really, and understandably cautious. After all, it's been over two years since they've even seen the lad. And there's no knowing how they'll bond when they do.'

'Well, this all sounds positive, at least,' I said, glancing across to the living area. 'And I suppose it also means that ours will potentially be a short placement.

And for all the right reasons, of course. Am I right in thinking that because it's grandparents the whole process is faster than normal?'

'Hopefully,' Lydia said. 'At least, if all goes well, then yes. Let's just hope there are no more skeletons in the extended family cupboard and that it's all pretty straightforward. In the meantime, just do as you're doing, try and keep his mood up, and in a few days I'll have some more information to share, because we will need to get him into a school. And local to you, I think because that's going to be easier for everyone, even if it means moving again in a few months. For one thing, he needs his education and, for another, he'll come along a lot faster emotionally if he is around other kids and has that routine.'

I agreed wholeheartedly – it almost felt as if she was putting my very thoughts into words – and after she said a quick goodbye to Ethan, Lydia left me to it. I closed the door behind her and looked at the suitcase and bags, all full, presumably, of the minutiae of the boy's life. His *former* life, I mentally corrected, with a pang of sorrow. His toys, clothes and books. His special things.

But it wasn't going to be this kind of baggage that the poor child would lug around with him for years to come. It was the kind of emotional baggage that none of us wanted to carry. I picked it all up and made my unsteady way up the stairs with it. Fingers crossed we could help lighten it some.

Chapter 5

My first supervising social worker and good friend John Fulshaw was a great reader and would often share quotes with me. One of his favourites, and a famous one, penned by the author Leo Tolstoy, was 'All happy families are alike; each unhappy family is unhappy in its own way'.

John reckoned that quote worked for children as well; though, depressingly, we saw the same scenarios over and over – drug and alcohol addiction, abuse, violence and neglect – every child reacted slightly differently to the traumas they'd suffered. Some lashed out at others, some withdrew into themselves, others displayed behaviours that were chaotic and often challenging, and a few left us baffled and scratching our heads.

Which was all to be expected – there are few things in nature more complex than the human brain, after all – so I knew it was only going to be a matter of time before the true nature of little Ethan was revealed to us. But I perhaps didn't expect it quite as quickly – or dramatically – as the very next morning.

As far as I knew, he'd slept through the night; he'd certainly been asleep when I looked in on him late evening, and again in the small hours when I got up to use the loo. But when I went into his room to wake him up the following morning, what I found there was something of a shock.

After Lydia, Ethan's social worker, had left us the previous day, we'd spent much of the afternoon sorting through and putting away his belongings; in the wardrobe, in the toy box and in the drawers. He'd been quiet, almost on a kind of autopilot as we'd done this, offering nothing in the way of commentary about *why* we were doing it and, taking his matter-of-fact lead, I didn't push it. The time would come, soon enough, when his world would implode, and all I could do was be there to catch him when he fell.

Was this evidence of that fall? Because when I looked into the bedroom pretty much everything that we had put away so nicely, all his clothes and books and toys, seemed now to be strewn around everywhere. Most notably, his half dozen assorted teddies had been thrown from the bed and adjacent window ledge, and, most surprising of all, his three treasured *Paw Patrol* vehicles now lay in pieces on his bedside table.

Ethan, still in bed, was sitting up and glaring. 'I hate them!' he yelled. Had he been waiting for me to enter?

I was startled. Even though I anticipated it coming, I hadn't heard such raw anger in his voice before. 'I don't want this stuff!' he shouted. 'It's some other boy's stuff! Mine's at my *mummy's*!' He practically screamed the last word.

Trying to counter his rage with calm, I began picking up clothes, placing them back in the still-open drawers, while wondering about the best way to play things. Logic seemed to suggest that I go over and try to comfort him, but some instinct was telling me no. At least not yet; he was like a very tightly wound spring, and my hunch was that a cuddle was only likely to make things worse. I went with the instinct. 'No, Ethan, this is all your stuff, love,' I said mildly. 'You know it is, because that nice lady, Lydia, brought it over for you yesterday. And I'm putting it all back because you need your clothes to wear. And what about these teddies?' I added, picking up the closest two and approaching the bed with them. And it was at this point that I noticed the smell.

My mind recoiled then. Surely not? But there was now no mistaking it. It came at my nostrils like a juggernaut as Ethan pulled up his legs.

'Sweetie,' I asked him. 'Have you had an accident in your bed?'

In response, Ethan whipped back the duvet. I couldn't help but gag at the stench that now mushroomed up between us, and gape at the state he was in. He'd removed his pyjama bottoms and was absolutely covered in poop, from his waist down to his feet. I then noticed his hands, which were smeared with poop too. It was also all over the sheet and the duvet cover.

'Oh, Ethan!' I couldn't help but exclaim. 'Why have you done that, love? Why didn't you go to the bathroom?'

It was a stupid question. As if any child of his age would know why they'd done it. It might have been an accident – at least started as an accident. But what he'd done subsequently … that was a *whole* other matter. I crossed the room and flung the window open to let some fresh air in, but as I did so, he bolted from the bed and ran out of the room. Conscious of what he was covered in, I quickly followed, hoping to stop him before he started touching anything, silently cursing as I realised the soles of his feet were in the same state.

'Ethan,' I called, 'stop! I need to get you cleaned up.'

To which he responded with a 'Fuck you!' slung back over his shoulder, which shocked me almost as much as what he'd done. Doesn't matter how many times you are faced with such profanities, hearing an expression like that, yelled in anger, from the mouth of a five-year-old can never be anything but deeply depressing, because it was a signifier for so much that was wrong.

Ethan ran into the bathroom and slammed the door before I could stop him and then, even as I had my hand on the handle, I heard the bolt slipping into the lock. I could have cried then, surveying the scene of devastation. There was poo smeared along the landing handrail, and the bathroom door and door jamb, and streaks of it on my new pale grey carpet. And it hit me in the same way that the stench from the bed had; was this simply a reaction to his mother's tragic death, or was it more than that? Was this a manifestation of the real Ethan? His mother's death aside, was this evidence of an already psychologically challenged child?

Another child, another little boy, came to mind. Seth. Who I'd looked after not so very long ago. He'd come as part of a package – we looked after both him and his mum and newborn baby brother – and, by any yardstick, his behaviours had been what is generally termed as 'challenging'. And, sometimes, the professional terminology we use doesn't quite do justice to the thing they are attempting to describe.

All this flashed through my mind as I knocked on the bathroom door. That and what had happened made my heart sink for another reason. His grandparents would have no idea of potentially what they might be taking on. Would they have the skills and patience to deal with the challenges? Would they even *want* to?

'Ethan,' I called, 'you need to open this door for me, okay? So I can come in and help you after you've used the toilet. You've got poo everywhere, sweetheart, and it's not a problem – you're not in any trouble – but I do need to get in there so I can help clean it all up.'

There was no reply but I could hear the toilet flushing and then the sound of taps running. 'Ethan, love,' I called again. 'Can you please unlock the door for me?',

45

but though I tried several times, over the course of several minutes, all I could hear was the still-running taps and the sound of cupboards opening and closing. My softly, softly approach was clearly not working. A change of tack was obviously needed here.

'Ethan!' I said again, this time *much* more firmly. 'I won't ask you again, young man. Open this door, please!'

Silence. The sound of movement stopped. This voice he *was* listening to. 'I mean it,' I said. 'I am going to count to three now. And that door best be opened. One … two …'

I heard the bolt being pulled back and suddenly, there he was. Standing in the doorway and – what was that? Was he *grinning* at me?

'See, I told you I could do it,' he announced, though he hadn't. 'See? I'm clean now. And I'm hungry. Can I have some breakfast?'

Beyond the unlikely, half-dressed, not quite clean child in the doorway, I could see my fluffy pink bath towel in a heap on the floor, wet through and covered with streaks of the offending stuff. The toilet seat and basin were both smeared with it too. So he'd obviously *tried*, but had only succeeded in making things worse.

Plastering a smile on my own face, I told him well done for trying, but that breakfast would still have to wait a bit. 'Because first,' I pointed out, keeping my voice pretty firm still, 'I am going to run some water in the bottom of the bath, and you are going to stand in it, and between us and a sponge and some of my very best magic bubbles, we are going to clean you down properly. Understand?'

Thankfully, he didn't argue. Maybe his growling stomach had taken precedence over his defiance. I didn't know. There would be time for analysis later. Though as I stripped his top off and sponged him down, he offered a kind of explanation. 'I dunno why I did that,' he said. 'I knew I needed a poo. But I forgot where the toilet was, cos I don't live here, do I? An' then I ...' He tailed off then and shrugged.

'And then?' I prompted.

He shrugged again. 'I dunno. I s'pose I went back to sleep.' And that was it, so, again, I decided not to push it. I wasn't sure the explanation was the whole story – far from it, was my guess – but it was a can of worms I decided not to open for now. Best just to take him at his word and let it go.

Which seemed to be the right approach. When we went back into his room to choose some clothes he made no mention of the mess, even joking about the poo smell – my bears are now all pooh bears! – and being biddable and compliant as I helped him to dress, reminding me once again that he was more like a three-year-old than a five-year-old. So perhaps this was all a part of that.

In any event, it wasn't long before he was seated at the breakfast bar with toast and cereal, and, having given him the children's tablet I'd inherited from my granddaughter Dee Dee (with a 'What is the world coming to?' grin from my son Kieron), I could get on with the business of going back upstairs to strip his bed and, hopefully, get the stains out of my carpet. Not to mention try to process what all this might mean.

And, as the day went on, a clearer picture began taking shape, evidence amassing that the little boy now in our care was likely to be more complex than he'd first seemed. Playing out in the garden, after breakfast, he'd knocked over a beautiful planter, causing it to smash and ruin the pelargoniums that had been growing there. An accident perhaps, but his maniacal laughter as I'd swept up the debris was unsettling indeed. Then at lunchtime, he'd 'accidentally' upended his bowl of tomato soup then refused point-blank to help me clear the mess up. Back in the garden, after lunch, he'd then repeatedly kicked a ball at the garden mirror Mike had placed at the back of one of the borders, till he'd managed (I didn't doubt by this time that it was deliberate) to create a long jagged crack down the middle of it.

Having had such a 'mare of a day' with Ethan (as my daughter Riley would have put it), I decided that tiring him out would be the best thing. Though unable to articulate it, he was clearly acting out due to distress, and if there was little I could do to change his current situation, at least I could help ensure that he got sufficient sleep, by bringing on some good old-fashioned physical exhaustion, via a nice long walk.

At the end of that, however, it was me who was exhausted, Ethan proving even more of a challenge than in close confinement at home. He kept running off and refusing to hold my hand as we crossed roads, meaning I had to grab him by the back of his hoodie, while he writhed around and cussed, wearing me out – he was definitely stronger than he looked – and making us a spectacle to every passer-by. By the time we returned from our trek round the suburbs, all I had the energy to do about tea was pick up my laptop and order takeaway pizza from Uber Eats.

Which arrived just as Mike walked through the door. 'This a treat?' he asked when we finally got settled down to eat.

'This is actually just me giving in,' I said. 'After the day I've had, I have neither the time nor the inclination to start cooking.' Or, indeed, I thought, the inclination to practise diplomacy, however sorry I felt for the boy. However grim the circumstances – actually, *because* of the circumstances – some boundaries would need establishing, and soon.

Mike, who had still to be debriefed, grinned at Ethan. 'You been giving my Casey a hard time today, kiddo?'

Ethan shook his head. 'I've been a good boy all day,' he said, a sweet smile spreading across his face.

To which Mike responded by ruffling the boy's hair. 'Good lad,' he said. 'You eat all your tea up, then me and you will go out back for a kickabout. How's that sound?'

Sounds bloody brilliant, I thought, *now there's nothing left to break, my nerves included*. But I smiled. At least

Ethan could let off some more steam, and I'd have a little time to decompress. And to think. Which I continued to do all that evening. Mostly about what kind of child we'd taken in and how much of what I'd seen could be attributed to his loss – and how much was the child Ethan was. Because instinct was telling me that certain things I'd seen in Ethan *were* ingrained, an integral part of who he was. Not his fault, not at all. A child of five doesn't choose to behave badly; they just don't know how to act any differently to what they are used to. Not if they come from a background of few rules or boundaries, and really don't understand social expectations. And with his mother having died of a heroin overdose, there was a pretty good chance, a probability, even, that Ethan had come from such a home.

I could only hope that this wasn't Ethan's story, obviously. But chances were that it was, at least to some degree, anyway. Which left me sad, desperately sad, for him but also resolute. With this child, rather than fight to get beneath the behaviours and tackle the root causes myself, I would leave that to the other professionals who would now, or hopefully soon, be in his life. I would accept that, this time, my job would be to support and to socialise, to treat him as the toddler his behaviours suggested his true emotional age was. I would teach him right from wrong and how to behave acceptably around others, show him love, understanding, patience and compassion, model decent behaviours and, above all, set those boundaries. And, most important of all, I would ensure they were adhered to. I couldn't bring his mum back but I could use my skills to help mould him into a child who would be liked and accepted, particularly by his peers, and so have a decent shot at future happiness; not least because his grandparents taking him in might depend on that very thing.

That, I concluded, was the very best I could do for him. It wasn't rocket science to do that, but it did share a common trait with it; the constant possibility of there being spanners in the works. I had no idea what size or shape those spanners might be, obviously, but I'd be as ready as I could for them.

Or so I thought.

Chapter 6

Ethan, it seemed, had more than a few spanners to throw in the works. In fact, he had an entire toolbox! The night terrors started within a few days, and they were something to behold. As terrifying as they must have been for poor Ethan, for me, witnessing this half-asleep, half-awake nightmare state he was in, it was almost like getting a glimpse inside his mind. Harrowing, but at the same time, almost mesmerising.

The first time it happened was obviously the most distressing, as it was presaged by a scream of an ear-splitting intensity the like of which I'd never heard outside a horror movie.

It was just after 3.00 a.m. and I immediately leapt out of bed, rushing along the landing with my heart pumping furiously, the adrenalin already coursing through my arteries. Surely such a tiny human couldn't even *make* such a noise? And I had looked after a *lot* of tiny humans.

But he could and he was. I flung open his bedroom door to find the covers kicked back and Ethan himself rigid with terror. His head and feet and legs were still flat on the bed, but his entire torso was arched towards the ceiling. It put me in mind of something I'd read about how people died from strychnine poisoning, even though Ethan, still screaming, was very much alive.

'Christ, it looks like a scene out of *The Exorcist*!'

I swung my head around. I hadn't realised Mike was behind me.

'Is he awake?' he added, raising his voice to be heard over the screaming.

Ethan's eyelids were fluttering, allowing me to inter-mittently see that his eyes were rolled back into his head. I hadn't witnessed anything like this before so I wasn't exactly sure what to do. All I did know, presum-ably from some long-ago training lecture, was that we shouldn't startle him into waking while still in this state.

'He's had a nightmare,' I told Mike. 'And by the looks of things, still is. I think the softly, softly approach is what's needed here.'

I padded across the room, and started to stroke Ethan's head. With just the very lightest of touches. He was clammy with sweat. 'Shhh ...' I began whispering. 'Shhh ... it's okay, sweetie. You're alright, Ethan. Shhh. You've just had a bad dream.'

The screaming had stopped almost as soon as my hand had touched his head, and now, little by little, the rigidity softened, till he was once more inert and apparently asleep still on the bed, though from the gentle whimpers I could hear, he was waking.

It was then that I noticed a large stain beginning to bloom on the front of his *Paw Patrol* pyjama bottoms.

'He's just lost control, that's all,' I said to Mike, by way of explanation. 'Love, go back to bed. You need your sleep. I'll sort this out.'

I was also aware that, in his confused distressed state, Ethan might fare a little better if it was just me he saw. He was used, after all, to it just being him and his mother. Which thought immediately brought a prickle to my throat. It was his mother who should be here when he woke from a nightmare; it was one of those fundamental constants of childhood. Now lost to him. It was heartbreaking to even think about.

Mike ran his hand through his wild night-time hair. I knew he wouldn't argue. 'If you're sure, love. I've got a busy day coming up so I could do with another couple of hours.'

I watched Mike head off, feeling guilty that he'd been woken in the first place. He wasn't old, nowhere near, but he wasn't young either. If he didn't get his sleep, I'd begun to notice, it increasingly affected his day. Mind you, I thought, as I continued to soothe Ethan, those screams were loud enough to wake half the street, especially as the small top windows were open. What must our new neighbours be thinking?

Making a mental note to find an opportunity to let the closest ones know we were foster carers, I turned back to Ethan, who was fully coming round now, presumably in part because he'd have felt the warm wetness.

I perched on the edge of the bed and smiled down at him. 'You had a bad dream, darling, but you're all okay now. We just need to get you out of those wet things, okay? Let's do that, shall we? And change that wet sheet.'

'I had an accident?' he asked, sleepily. Then, without pausing, 'There was blood and a bad man was stabbing my mummy. I want Mummy. I want my mummy. And my daddy. I want my daddy!'

He started to cry again, this time noisily, distressed and fully conscious, so, instinctively really, as I'd been so careful not to crowd him, I reached out to hug him, as anyone would and, to my surprise he scooted straight into my open arms. He then buried his damp head into my chest as he wept.

'Why can't I see him?' he sobbed. 'I've been a good boy. Why can't I *see* him?'

The lump in my throat made it difficult for me to answer for a moment. It was just all so wretched, so upsetting. And, despite myself, an unbidden wave of anger washed over me, towards the mother that had allowed her need for drugs to outweigh her responsibility for her son.

I tried to quash it; I knew things were unlikely to ever be as simple as that, and I knew almost nothing of his mother's story. But *as* a mother I couldn't help that deep-rooted maternal anger. Because, on some level, it was still true, wasn't it? Certainly, for Ethan, growing up, it would *feel* true. It would take a lot of work and support to help him process that sense that she hadn't loved him quite enough to stay alive for him – it made little difference if it was justified or not.

All of which rambling thoughts would not help him much now. He needed comfort and to know his needs were being listened to.

'You *are* a good boy, sweetie,' I eventually said. 'And I promise you, cross my heart, that first thing in the morning I will phone someone and find out when you can see your daddy. That's a promise,' I said again. 'And your grandma and grandad. I will ask about you seeing them too.'

Ethan looked up at me then, his eyes huge and bright with tears still. 'Grannie Jo and Pops?'

I nodded. I wasn't aware of any other grandparents on the scene at all. 'Your mummy's mummy and daddy,' I confirmed.

'But I'm not allowed so see them,' he said. 'Because they're shit-bags.'

I was momentarily stunned. Both at the words he used – clearly a repetition of ones that had been drilled into him – and, more than that (and in a better way), at the confusion, and sudden hope, I could now see in his expression as he recalibrated the world view he'd been given. Honestly, the damage some people caused their kids was horrendous.

'Yes, you are,' I said gently, skipping past any clarification – this wasn't the time to attempt to discuss why. 'They want to see you, darling, and they are very, very nice. Pops has been a bit poorly – that's why you haven't seen them for a long while, but he's feeling much better now, and can't wait to see you again.'

I didn't know whether that statement was true or would turn out to be fiction, but I didn't care. This boy needed to know someone wanted him in their lives and that he had a family that would make him feel safe.

I scooped Ethan up now and quickly stripped off his wet pyjamas, and, perhaps with his mind full of new possibilities, he let me take charge and get it done. Then, because of the time it was, I opted not to wash him. I simply popped on clean jim-jams (again, he just allowed it, his little hands resting warmly on my shoulders as he stepped into the bottoms) and decided to do something I hadn't in years. Instead of stripping the bed, I went to the airing cupboard and grabbed a huge bath towel and a sheet, then went back, folded the former and placed it over the wet patch, topping it off with the latter, and popping Ethan back in bed. It wasn't like me to be so slapdash, but it would *do*.

'I'll sort all the bedding out tomorrow,' I told him. 'You try to get back to sleep now. I'll leave the door open and the landing light on, okay?' I then stooped to kiss his head, upon which his arms snaked round my neck again, and he held me there, tightly, for some seconds.

'Night, Casey,' he whispered finally, as he released me. And it was only as I padded out of the room that it hit me that it was the first time he had called me by my name. So, a nightmare, but also a breakthrough.

I never did get back to sleep that night, my mind motoring on in overdrive, trying to work out the possible meaning behind what Ethan had said about blood and stabbing and bad men. In the absence of any facts, the only thing I could come up with was that he was too young to understand what death meant. He couldn't make sense of finding his mummy looking like she was asleep on the floor, and then being told she had died. Perhaps his subconscious brain had been searching for explanations, and he'd probably seen something on TV – maybe a movie, or the news even – about a stabbing and blood, and had turned his mother's death into a scene that he could accept as being final. Perhaps a bloody massacre, to Ethan, meant death. Not the scene he had actually witnessed.

The next morning, though, Ethan made no mention of the previous night's trauma. I did as I had promised and made the calls that would hopefully bring forward some family visits. Thankfully, Christine had agreed with me, and by the Thursday it was arranged that on that Sunday, and, going forward, every other Sunday, a family support worker would come to collect Ethan and take him on a prison visit to see his dad. Even better news was that 'Grannie' had agreed to contact twice-weekly, supervised in a family centre across town, and that would start just as soon as Mr Baines was a little more mobile and over his surgery.

So, we were getting somewhere. Hopefully inching towards a full family reconciliation, with both his dad, and the grandparents who'd been expunged from his life in goodness-knows-what kind of circumstances. 'Though it will be just Grandma for the first two sessions,' Christine explained, 'and then, if it goes well, Grandad will be joining them. Mrs Baines wants to test the waters on her own first to see how it goes.'

'Did it have to be in a contact centre?' I asked. 'I mean, is there any reason for that?'

'Grandma requested that,' Christine said. 'There's no background stuff come to light that would prevent unsupervised access, but she says she wants some support in place while she sees Ethan in case she can't manage it. I suppose she's a bit wary really, given that they haven't seen each other in such a long time, and she doesn't know what to expect – not least how he'll respond to seeing her.'

I nodded, impressed, when I thought about it, that the grandmother seemed to be taking things at a sensible pace. 'I suppose it's the right thing to do,' I conceded, 'and I'm so pleased for Ethan. I really hope it goes well, for his sake.'

I then filled Christine in a bit about the conclusions I had drawn regarding Ethan's bad dreams, and his representation of death, and again, Christine agreed with me. She said she would pass it all on to Lydia Heptonstall, so that when the dreadful work started, she at least had a point of reference to go from.

Ethan was over the moon when I told him about the upcoming visits. So much so that I learned a valuable lesson for the future: that I should wait till the last minute to give him such news. Over the next couple of days, he would grill me about ten times an hour. 'How many days before I see Daddy? How many hours does that make?' And then, when I told him, 'Oh my God! That's too many hours! I *hate* hours!'

On the Saturday, to avoid my going completely insane by this constant countdown, I decided I'd risk taking Ethan into town to get us both out of the house and hopefully distract him from his anguished waiting.

'You have pocket money to spend,' I said, bigging up the excitement. 'Maybe we could buy some special colours and cards and things so you can make something for Daddy. And for Grannie Jo and Pops too. What do you think?'

'Yes!' Ethan yelled as he jumped up and down. 'And a toy too? Did you get your versacredit?'

It took less than a second to work out what 'versa-credit' was. Universal Credit was the relatively new name for unemployment benefits, but it was both funny and sad that Ethan thought I'd just been paid this. Wow, though, so young and he already understood the relationship between getting bought things and waiting for benefits. On the one hand, I suppose it's a good lesson that children need to know they have to wait until the adults in their lives get paid before getting treats. But it was also sad that a child as young as Ethan knew what that money was called, because surely, I thought, as he grew up, that knowledge would be the only thing he knew as normal. Trust me, I don't look down on anyone who has to use the benefits system in order to survive, especially young mothers who have no family network that would enable them to go out to work. I just think it's a sad state of affairs that more support isn't in place to help these people overcome the hurdles of ridiculously expensive childcare, and to be able to find real, worthwhile job opportunities.

But that was a conversation for a far-away day. I ruffled Ethan's hair. 'Go grab your coat then, kiddo. It's chilly out there. Let's go spend some of my money, eh?'

I was silently praying that, because of his high spirits, Ethan would behave better in the outside world than he had the last time we went out. That he'd hold my hand without dragging me, and cross roads with me sensibly, but, as often happened where children were concerned, my perhaps unrealistic prayers went unanswered. He was only five, after all, and a young five at that. There would, I knew, be a long way to go.

In the meantime, every shop seemed to be a 'free-for-all', at least as far as Ethan was concerned. He'd slip away from me at every opportunity, running off and hiding behind racks or window displays, and giggling manically when I discovered him and tried rootling him back out. It really was very stressful, especially when I got those looks from sales assistants; those ones that said, 'What kind of a grandmother must she be, allowing her grandkid to run riot like that?'

I got through it as best I could and did manage to pick up some art and craft materials. We did already have a huge tub full of stuff at home, obviously, but each time a new child entered our lives, it invariably got added to. And with good reason; I knew that they felt some ownership of the tub once their own bits and pieces were added to it.

By the time I was ready to head back to the car, I was well and truly hot and bothered. The cold October air doing nothing to cool me down, and I reminded myself once again that I really must speak to Christine about pushing for that school place so I would at least have time to do some solo shopping.

'Come on then,' I cajoled Ethan, 'let's get these bags back to the car and get home.' It was then I remembered that I had promised Riley that, if I went into town, I'd nip into a clothes shop and pick up some socks for her boys, Levi and Jackson. Men's sizes now, too! It was unbelievable how much those grandsons of mine had grown; they both towered over me these days. 'Oh, I just have one last shop to nip into,' I said, once we got outside the local market arcade, 'just for some socks. We'll only be two minutes.'

Surprisingly, Ethan conformed and grabbed hold of my outstretched hand.

'Last one,' he said, 'and I know how long two minutes is so I'm counting in my brain, okay?'

'Okay,' I said, grinning. I'd already forgotten not to put a time on anything unless I seriously exaggerate it.

What I'd also forgotten was Ethan's bad dream, and that proved to be a traumatic error on my part. We'd barely stepped onto the first aisle when Ethan started howling. I mean, real howling, like an injured animal. I felt him stiffen and the grip on my hand became vice-like, and then the screams started again. I glanced around the store, seeing both customers and staff staring, but for the life of me I couldn't understand what was happening. Without letting go of his hand, I knelt down in front of Ethan and tried to make eye contact with him.

'Ethan! What is it? What's wrong, sweetheart?' I asked him, aware that I was practically shouting to be heard by him, and the object of increasingly anxious attention. I shook his hand gently. 'I want to help you, Ethan, but you have to tell me what's wrong,' I continue. 'Ethan please, sweetie, tell me. What is it?'

With his free hand, Ethan pointed ahead towards the middle of the aisle, 'B … b … b … blood!' he screamed. 'Blood!'

Bewildered, I looked to where he was indicating and then it hit me. Bloody Halloween costumes! I mean, *literally* bloody. A whole rack of zombie clothing, splatted liberally with red paint, and, next to those, doctor and nurse outfits, similarly splattered. It came to me in a rush then. His *dream*. His only feasible interpretation of the death of his mummy. I couldn't beat myself up about it, because why on earth *would* this have occurred to me? Still, it saddened me, not least because I hadn't even realised it was almost Halloween. Riley's socks would have to wait, I decided, as I scooped Ethan up without asking him – luckily he allowed it and didn't kick off. 'Come on, kiddo,' I said, my arms killing me with all the bags and now a child to carry too. 'They're just silly, joke outfits, and that's just red paint, sweetheart. Let's get you home and we can do some nice pictures. Get these horrible ones out of your head, okay?'

But I couldn't help wondering if getting them out of his head was going to be pretty hard to do.

Chapter 7

I had been so, so lucky as a foster carer, to have such brilliant supervising social workers – or link workers as they used to be called. John Fulshaw had been my first, and we worked together for many years. He 'got me', as I used to say to Mike all the time, and it was very clear that he was in it for the kids, and to facilitate change in the service where it was needed. I was devastated when he left to follow his career dreams – a role higher up in the service, the better to be able push through those important changes – and was dreading who I might be assigned after him.

I needn't have worried, though, because Christine Bolton was just as brilliant, just as down to earth and just as passionate about her job. So much so that, unlike many managers, she instinctively understood that when we had children in, and they weren't in school, the only opportunity we usually had to really talk and share our worries was after they went to bed. It was for this reason that I had Christine's private numbers, as well as her work ones – both her home one and her personal mobile. I never abused the privilege and only ever called those numbers unless I absolutely had to, but after that day in town with Ethan, I felt it was one of those times.

'Poor little sod,' Christine said after I'd explained what had happened. 'And you're absolutely right, Casey, it's imperative that we get him stabilised as soon as possible. Get him some routine in his life, and yes, school will obviously be the priority. I'll get onto them first thing on Monday morning, I promise.'

'That would be great,' I said, 'it's like bloody Groundhog Day for him at the moment. Bad night's sleep, nightmares, then a day spent just with me. And it's usually indoors, with me trying everything I can to keep him occupied, then it's eat, sleep, repeat. The kid is bound to be going a bit stir-crazy, so it's no wonder he acts out the minute we go somewhere different. Same for me too, to be honest. I know it's only been a short time but, oh, what I'd give for a leisurely stroll around the bloody supermarket!'

Christine laughed. 'Well, on that front, I can be your fairy godmother. I was going to phone you in the morning anyway but, well, your wish is my command, Casey. As you know, his family support worker, Heather Wilkins, will be coming to collect Ethan at 9.15 tomorrow morning to go and visit his dad, but what you didn't know – because I must confess I didn't either – was that it's for a full day, not a couple of hours like we thought.

It usually starts off with shorter visits, but then it builds up, so I'm told, the closer the prisoner gets to their release date. Plus, it's a two-hour drive, apparently, and once they get there, they'll be going straight for something to eat. The visit is actually from 11.30 till 3.30 and I'm told Ethan is given a snack afterwards, and then, like I said, it will be around 6.00 p.m. by the time they get back. So you might want to pack some extra bits and bobs for him.'

I could feel myself smiling down the phone. 'Yes, of course. And, oh, wow,' I said, 'a whole day to myself! And yay for Ethan, bless him – getting all that time with his dad. Christine, this is *great* news. You have made my day now, truly. Thank you!'

'Hold up a minute,' Christine added quickly. 'Not so much a *whole* day – well, at least, not if you agree. I know Sundays can be sacrosanct, so please say no if you want to, but I was thinking I could come through to see you for an hour or so while Ethan's not there. There's a very complicated story I have to share with you about Brogan, his mother. I've had some very long and interesting conversations with his grandmother, Jocelyn, and, well, like I say, the background is quite complicated, and I'd sooner tell it to you face to face. You up for that?'

Even as Christine had been speaking I was already nodding my 'yes', even if she couldn't see it down the phone. I was always so aware of her own personal situation. Having lost her only child to cot death and, lately, her husband's dad (who I knew had taken up a lot of her and her husband's time), I wondered what the weekends were like for her. We were roughly the same age and when I thought of how full of family my own life was – how there never seemed a moment when I wasn't doing something with, or chatting to, or organising fun times for one or other of them – I couldn't quite imagine what Christine got up to when not in work. She never spoke of any wider family, or of having any hobbies, and I knew just how committed she was to her job, but I also knew that, beneath her usually upbeat demeanour, there must be a sadness, and a grief, that would never leave her.

Of course, I could have been barking up the wrong tree; maybe she and her husband had a high old time, enjoying dining out at fancy restaurants, and going on city breaks or whatnot, but she was such an obviously maternal woman – it was why she did what she did, after all – that instinct told me otherwise. So of course she'd be happy to visit me on a Sunday.

As was I. Because I did always love a mystery. I was almost salivating at the thought of delving into this one, and my investigatory senses were already spiking. In my line of work, information about a child's background was so incredibly important, after all, especially if it had badly impacted on their psyche. Which was, of course, true of most of the children we took in.

'Are you kidding me?' I said. 'Of course I'm up for it, Chris! Mike doesn't call me "inch-high private eye" for nothing, you know.'

Christine laughed loudly. 'I thought as much. Right then, I'll see you at around 9.30 a.m., so you can have the rest of the day to yourself. Have the kettle ready. I'll need at least two pots of tea.'

So I woke up on Sunday morning in a bright, positive mood. Ethan had done some pictures the previous evening, just as I'd suggested, including one of another *Paw Patrol* character (I'd drawn him the outline) which he was particularly proud of and which was destined for his dad. And, perhaps because he'd gone to bed knowing it was his last sleep before going to see him, he had slept like a top, at least as far as I could tell. No screams, no dramas, no reports of any nightmares, and when I'd gone in to wake him, I swear he didn't seem to have moved a muscle since I'd checked on him before going to bed myself.

Mike too was in a good mood. He generally was on any day that involved the words 'Kieron' and 'football'. They were off to watch a match between two teams in the local league and he was out of the door, whistling to himself, before I was even dressed. And, of course, little Ethan was in an excited mood too, bubbling over with fizz and questions as I dressed him in the smart new skinny jeans and sweater that, despite all the drama, I had managed to buy him the day before.

'Am I going to live with Daddy,' he asked, as I wriggled his trainers onto his feet, 'in his big, big house?'

His big, big house; I guessed that was a helpful way to process the prison for him. I shook my head. 'No, darling, not live there, but you *are* going to spend the whole day with him, and after that, you will be going lots and lots of times to see him, right up to when he comes out of his, um, big, big house.'

Ethan bounced his bottom on the sofa in excitement. 'And *then* I'm going to live with him? In his new house? Will that be a big house as well?'

I didn't really want this conversation to go the way it was going, and I definitely didn't want to make any promises that couldn't be kept, but neither did I want to ruin the poor boy's enthusiasm about his possible future. This was the first time he'd ever spoken about anything other than the immediate moment, and in my opinion it needed to be encouraged. Not least because it felt like the first tangible evidence that he was processing his mother's death. At least it seemed so.

'Well, sweetie,' I said carefully, 'nobody can be certain about what might happen in the future, because we can't see into the future, can we? But hopefully everything will turn out just right for you, and you will be a very happy little boy. How does that sound?'

Ethan considered me then, his gaze unwavering, his expression thoughtful. 'It sounds good, Casey,' he said, nodding. 'My daddy makes me happy, an' he told me that when he comes home we can make 'pagetti bollock naked together.'

I almost choked. 'You mean spaghetti *Bolognese*, Ethan,' I corrected, before swiftly changing the subject. I was sure I'd heard that said before but couldn't recall when, or who by. Probably Tyler ... It was definitely the kind of thing he'd say as a joke. I shook away the sudden pang the thought of Ty gave me. I couldn't wait to see him. I was happy for him but I missed him dreadfully. Specially his corny jokes.

'Let's get your coat on then, kiddo,' I said, pulling Ethan up from the sofa. 'And then you can watch out for the lady who's taking you to see Daddy while I get your backpack together.'

'Is it my lady Heather?' Ethan asked as he parked himself in front of the window to look out. 'She's nice to me and sometimes gets me sweeties from a massive machine at Daddy's big house.'

'I think it is,' I said as I zipped up his bag. 'I don't know for definite. But almost certainly, and I'm really happy to hear that she's nice to you.'

Within ten minutes, I would see that for myself. And with the picture he'd done for his daddy safely stashed in the backpack, along with some treats and a drink, Ethan and Heather were soon good to go. Extra good in Ethan's case, because Heather, who it turned out was indeed the same support worker who'd taken him on his prison visits before his mum's death, came bearing an iPad – his very own iPad, she assured him, with episodes of the shows he liked best already downloaded.

'Wow!' I said as Ethan fell upon the tablet in raptures of delight. 'Is that Ethan's to keep? Or did he already have one?'

Heather ruffled Ethan's hair, and I noted the easy affection between them. This relationship, this continuity, was good news indeed. 'Well, he used to have one,' she said, 'and he loves to watch it in the car, but his old one – don't ask me how or why – disappeared. Anyhow, I've been promising to bring him this for a while now. From before' – she frowned slightly – 'events overtook us. It's one that got handed back in when a child upgraded to a laptop, so we put all Ethan's favourite stuff on it for him. Including every episode of *Paw Patrol* we could find,' she added, grinning at him.

'Thanks, Hev,' Ethan said, grinning from ear to ear. Then to me, 'It's okay I call her Hev, don't I, Hev? And Hev Hev. But never Hevvy Hev. I'm not allowed to call her Hevvy Hev.' They both laughed then at what was obviously a shared joke.

And she clearly knew him well; they had hugged the very moment they saw each other, and if I'd had my way, I'd have asked her to pencil in a quick meeting with me too, so I could pick her brains about this complicated little boy.

But there was a lot to find out in any case, as Christine wouldn't be long arriving. Just time to down a second cup of coffee and have a quick tidy round downstairs. Which was already tidy – I *did* know that. But I couldn't not do it. Some people double-check their hair, others re-apply lipstick. Me, I plump cushions and straighten chairs. That done, at 9.29, I put the kettle on as instructed, then at nine thirty sharp – had she been lurking by the hedge? – Christine rang the doorbell. And I could tell just by her expression that it was going to be some story. One to which we already knew the tragic ending, of course, but also a big step on the road to understanding how the tragedy had come about.

And, hopefully, it would help us start to make things better.

Chapter 8

Ethan's mum, Brogan, was only twenty-five when she died. The tragedy was that she hadn't meant to. She loved her son and would never have intentionally robbed him of his mother, but it seemed she'd bought some unusually pure heroin from an unfamiliar dealer, the effects of which she never came round from. A lethal overdose, a killer substance.

Drugs had been Brogan's crutch over the past couple of years and though she'd always felt – and would maintain, anytime anybody challenged her – that she was in control of her addiction, and not vice versa, just like many, many young addicts before her, she hadn't noticed the correlation between her move to increasingly powerful and increasingly addictive substances and her life beginning the inevitable downward spiral.

At nineteen, however, life had been good for Brogan and her future had been looking pretty rosy. Still living at home with her parents, while completing a three-year course in travel and tourism at a local college, she had recently begun to plan what to do with her life. Part of this planning had taken her to a job interview at a stately home some twenty miles away; one that opened its doors to the public all year round. Her job would be to organise tours of the house and gardens, putting on special events, changing them up according to the season, and acting as contact point for schools and local councils, to sort out group bookings, arrange transport where needed and generally smooth out any wrinkles.

Brogan got the job, beating ten other shortlisted candidates, and, at this point, her self-esteem couldn't have been higher. She was riding high, she had achieved something and she had made her parents happy. They could not have been prouder that their little girl, their only child, was on the path to such a very bright future.

What no one could have predicted, though, was that this job would soon offer up something else. An alternative path, to which, like so many other young people, Brogan would allow her heart to lead the way. She started the new job just over a month after leaving college and within a few days she met a guy at work, Jack, one of the groundsmen, who she felt an immediate attraction for. He was a strong, hunky guy, tall and very good looking, but most of all he was kind and gentle, and made her laugh. Romance blossomed immediately and, after only a matter of weeks, Brogan told her parents she was moving in with him; that they had decided they were going to rent a house together in the village near the stately home. It made sense, after all – she'd be much closer to her work.

Her parents, obviously shocked by both the decision and the speed of it, counselled caution, to take a step back and wait for a bit. Besides, wouldn't it be better to concentrate on her career, and to stay at home and save up for a house deposit? And wasn't nineteen a little young to set up home with a lad she'd only known a matter of weeks? Over the next few weeks, the atmosphere at home grew more and more strained, as they continually pleaded with her to reconsider.

But Brogan, in love, would have none of it. And a few weeks later she moved into a cottage with her boyfriend, a boy they had met once, and knew nothing about, except for the bad feeling that settled upon them; the bright future they'd envisaged, of Brogan travelling the world, seemingly ripped away within a matter of months.

It was the cause of countless arguments, too. It wasn't their intention but every time Brogan went to visit them, acrimony became the order of the day. It could be sparked in an instant, by the most innocent of comments. Couldn't they see how ridiculous they sounded? And snobbish? Just because she was in love with someone who was 'only' a groundsman – as they'd unwisely put it – that didn't mean she couldn't still have her career. And they were being sexist, as well as classist, to even suggest it. She loved him and she didn't *care* how little they thought of him. Bit by bit, their relationship was deteriorating badly, her parents anxious not to provoke her, and to keep her on side, but equally anxious to try to get her to see sense – a task that was becoming increasingly futile. And by the time *they* had seen sense – realised that it was surely better to support her and to let this less than ideal relationship run its course – she had stopped coming round, after a big row with her dad, and was barely phoning either. Only once a week, to her mum, if they were lucky.

So, they waited it out, and they were right to. Jack, lovely as he was, had led a vastly different life to Brogan. Brought up bouncing around in care, after a short time with a mum who didn't love him, he had a complicated personality and was deeply insecure. As a result, within months the relationship *had* begun to break down, due to his claustrophobic levels of possessiveness and jealousy; he couldn't even bear to see Brogan so much as talking to another man. Things came to a head when, after seeing Brogan chatting to and giggling with a male colleague at work one day, he completely lost it and accused her of cheating on him. Despite her vehement denials, Jack ended up having a brutal, physical fight with the guy in question, which resulted in his immediate dismissal.

It was a last straw for Brogan, who was horrified by what he'd done. She'd grown up in a world where violence was never the answer, and was equally mortified to think about why he'd done it; she was not, and never would be, his possession. So, she asked him to move out – which he did, without so much as a single plea to stay, a promise to change, to prove his worth. Not anything. It was almost as if he considered trying pointless, so low was his sense of self-worth. He simply went, leaving the area and disappearing altogether, presumably to find work somewhere else.

But Brogan's parents' happiness at this state of affairs was short-lived. It was only a few weeks later that Brogan realised that she was pregnant with Jack's child. Her parents, dismayed and anxious, urged her to have a termination, saying to have a baby now, especially as a single mum, would finish her career and ruin her life. But, to their distress (and shock, given that she had split up with the baby's father, and had already said she had no intention of finding him and telling him), Brogan was adamant that she was going to keep it. She'd been a lonely child, and had never felt particularly close to her parents, and she was also stubborn – the more they begged her to have an abortion, the more she dug her heels in and refused to – almost, her mother thought, as if on principle.

Relations worsened further; hoping to give their daughter a dose of reality, and perhaps bring her round to the idea of a termination before it was too late, her parents practised what they saw as necessary 'tough love', and warned Brogan that if she continued down this path, they wouldn't be there to bail her out financially and provide free childcare. She had made her bed, they told her, and now she must lie in it.

The plan backfired, and spectacularly, too. Because Brogan, to their consternation, told them she didn't need them anyway. She would live her own life, the way *she* wanted to, and they would no longer be part of it. She also swore they would never see their grandchild.

Stunned and mortified by this escalation, and the horrible turn of events, the Baines could only reflect on what they'd done wrong to bring about such a change in their daughter. It felt so inexplicable; what had happened to her? Was it pregnancy hormones? On reflection – and there would be *lots* of time for reflection – Jocelyn realised that perhaps she had underestimated the strength of the feelings Brogan still had for Jack. Yes, she'd asked *him* to leave, but he hadn't tried to fight for her. Had she secretly hoped he would try to get her back? And the pregnancy would have only compounded her distress. Perhaps, Jocelyn reasoned, the simple truth might be that she would not terminate the pregnancy because the baby was Jack's and, despite everything, Brogan still loved him.

And, Jack – in Jocelyn's opinion, a dubious character – had been her daughter's first proper love. But what now? He was long gone, but even at a distance, he was unwittingly controlling, and changing her daughter's destiny. And alienating her from her family in the process.

The pregnancy passed, as far as Jocelyn knew, without drama; her only contact with her daughter being an occasional text, her requests to speak, to meet up, all ignored. Jocelyn still privately seethed at her husband. Had he not been so stubborn – he and Brogan were so alike, and had always clashed – perhaps they could have made better headway. But he persisted in his view that she would see sense eventually; that if they held the line, and their position, she would soon come running back to them, for solace and support. Plus, he wasn't going to be dictated to by his 'chit of a daughter'. Jocelyn knew better than to try to argue because she knew he too was hurting; most of Brogan's ire, and unpleasant comments, had been directed at him, and he was the kind of man who found it hard to forgive.

But in the end, he was right. Brogan worked up until the eighth month of her pregnancy, then took maternity leave, hoping to return and make enough to get by. But after Ethan was born, she decided she didn't want to go back to her well-paid full-time job after all. She wanted to be there, as much as possible, for her baby. She'd already applied for housing benefit and, with in-work benefits as well, she thought she could find something part-time instead. At least, that was if she could have a reconciliation with her parents, and persuade them to childmind their grandson for two days a week.

Jocelyn was naturally overjoyed to have her daughter back in her life, and fell in love with her little grandson on sight. She also only worked part-time herself, doing accounts at a local retailers, so, with a bit of juggling, they could definitely make it work. But to her dismay, her husband, though equally pleased to repair relations, felt rather differently about being an unpaid childminder for two days a week, especially as he'd been recently diagnosed with type 2 diabetes and was off work sick, and very far from being in the best of health.

'We can't do it,' he told Brogan, 'and it's not fair to ask it of us. We'll help out where we can, of course, but it's too much to expect of us. You need a decent job, a decent career, if you're going to give that little 'un a decent life. Not be scrabbling around, on minimum wage, and claiming benefits.'

That was his philosophy – that you made your own way – but it hadn't been just that. He confided to Jocelyn later, it was another strategy to try and help their daughter: tough love. Another wake-up call for Brogan, for whom he genuinely – they both did – wanted a better life. He was already anxious that she had thrown away her future, and was already going downhill, setting her sights, and her ambitions, ever lower. And he didn't want the pair of them to be her enablers.

They considered alternatives. Perhaps, if Brogan returned to the well-paid job she already had, Jocelyn *could* help out with childminding (as she so desperately wanted to), meaning the cost of a nursery would at least be reduced. Plus, the figures worked; they even sat down and figured it all out on paper. But as those early weeks passed, and the prospect of the return to work loomed, Brogan, exhausted and shocked by the weight of her responsibilities, was less and less inclined to return. It just all felt too much, and though she was grateful to be supported, she felt vulnerable, low and resentful. This was their *grandson*. How was it right that their help came with conditions? And didn't her own mum have the privilege of staying home to mother *her*?

This, then, became the real reality check. And though her father didn't spell it out, he didn't have to. She had made her own bed, and now she had to lie in it. And though he didn't say it, Brogan knew he was thinking it. This was the reality of life for a single mother. Though no one could regret the beautiful baby in their lives, she should never have gone ahead with the pregnancy.

Headstrong as ever, Brogan took it to the brink, with conditions of her own about her now three-month-old child. If they refused to support her to find some part-time work for two days a week, then they could forget about seeing Ethan at *all*.

Looking back, Jocelyn struggled to work out what went wrong – to pinpoint the moment it all became irreparable. Was it one of the many rows? Was it her husband's holier-than-thou barbs? Or was it that they'd failed to appreciate their daughter's mindset? That it was almost as if she had crossed a red line, her need to prove them wrong, and her pride, taking precedence – to show she could manage without them. They would never know. They could only regret – and at leisure, because once again Brogan cut herself off from them.

It was shortly after that that Brogan's journey into drugs began, following her move closer to town, into a small council property, and befriending her new neighbours, a young couple with two little ones of their own. Despite being young parents, they still managed to party most nights and it wasn't long before Brogan was making sure Ethan was sleeping and then nipping next door to drink and, after a while, to experiment with drugs as well. Suddenly life was beginning to look brighter. She had friends now, ones who didn't mind if she dropped Ethan off while she went shopping, or for the occasional night out, and better yet, when the little money she had had run out, they were always happy to stump up with the drugs and the booze that would sweep away the pressures of being a full-time, single mum.

This new lifestyle went on, undetected, for over two years. By now, her relationship with her parents a distant memory, Brogan was fully immersed in the life she had made for herself and her son. She was getting by on little money, had kind and generous friends and neighbours, and if she needed a little chemical help to find the fun and happiness in life, well, so be it. Who didn't sometimes? There would be time, she always told herself, to get back to work, once Ethan had started at school.

And that might have been the case, had Jack not re-entered her life. Had he not turned up on her doorstep, completely out of the blue, and found out just how Brogan was living. Plus, he wasn't stupid. She had a child. And after very little prevaricating (she was a little the worse for wear when he'd shown up) she admitted that the boy was his.

The night did not end well. A huge row ensued, in Brogan's case a drunken one, which only served to inflame Jack's anger further. He completely lost his rag, began screaming and yelling, and, when the police arrived, following a concerned call from another neighbour, was found apparently threatening her, with his hands around her neck. He was immediately arrested and charged with multiple offences, including GBH.

Fearing the complications of having Jack back in her life now, when urged to, Brogan agreed to press charges. She was over him now, and didn't want him back in the picture. Dad to Ethan or not, he couldn't lay any claim to him. Plus, she'd managed all this time alone, and unsupported, so she didn't need him stepping in now. The police agreed, convinced she was doing the right thing, and she was more than happy to comply.

Jack duly went to prison, and Brogan too was in the spotlight, because of statements Jack had made about her drug-taking and general lifestyle. She had to work hard to convince social services that she was fit to look after Ethan, and at one point it was mooted that she should reconcile with her parents, but that ship had sailed now and, in the end, she just managed to. Regular home visits were set up and a family support worker assigned to Brogan, so that if she ever needed any help or support with Ethan – with *anything* – all she had to do was ask for it. She never did, of course;

she didn't want anyone sniffing around, and she was bright: she knew exactly how to create the right atmosphere that would convince anyone in her home that her child wasn't at risk. That he was loved. That he was cared for.

Then, after just under a year, came the news that Jack, keen to make amends, wanted to play a part in Ethan's future life. Though Brogan wanted nothing more to do with him personally, she still felt bad about what had happened, and also realised it would at least give her a chance to have a regular break. So she agreed, and fortnightly visits to see him in prison were set up. A family support worker would assist with all the transportation, and once again Brogan believed her life was on track.

Sadly, however, it wasn't. Though necessarily curtailed a little, because of scrutiny by the social services, Brogan's recreational drug use had never stopped. In fact, if anything, now Ethan was older, and slightly easier, it got worse; her fortnightly Sundays off more often than not consisted of little else *but* drugs.

Brogan was now on a carousel she couldn't get off. A slow, but steady incline from weed, to cocaine, and now, finally, the drug of drugs, heroin. Her life was anything but on track, though every day was a journey that started the same way. She needed that first hit the moment she woke up, just to be able to present herself to the world as a 'normal' mum, and to manage her much-loved, but increasingly challenging son.

Then later, inevitably, the guilt would set in, and she'd need another hit to stop that. Heroin now had her in its grip like a vice, and she knew it. Feeling adrift from her parents and now mourning their loss, she was too full of shame to even think of approaching them and showing them the reality of what she'd become. Her only solace was to turn to her faithful chemical friend, and she became increasingly dependent on the relief, the mental respite, heroin gave her. Just as Ethan needed her, she needed *it*.

The night Brogan died was apparently unremarkable. In the aftermath it was concluded that this was no isolated incident. There was no evidence whatsoever that she had meant to harm herself, that she would ever think, even for a second, of leaving her cherished son. No, the night Brogan died was just one among many when she'd put her boy to bed, then drifted off into oblivion, not knowing that, this time, she would never wake up.

Chapter 9

The tragic tale told, we sat in silence for a bit, while I digested what Christine had told me. It felt only right to let the words settle, to pay Brogan due respect, though it was as much a lack of words on my part as anything. All deaths are sad, but many, even a majority, tend to inspire words of comfort; a person in pain being freed from pain finally, a long life ended, but with happy memories to be cherished. A life celebrated. The normal cycle of birth and death to be accepted. Some deaths, though, were so tragic that there was no comfort to be had. This was one such – such a sad death, no question.

I knew Christine, all talked out, was happy to watch and wait, at least till she rose to refill the kettle. I was still in that room, crouched down beside that sobbing child, as stricken as he was to find his mum unresponsive and unable to believe that what had happened had happened. That she was never going to wake up. That she had gone.

And it *was* hard to process. Forget preconceived ideas about 'druggies' and 'irresponsible mums', this was a tragedy of Shakespearean proportions. If this story was true, and I had no doubt that it was, the whole sorry tale, from start to end, had left a family in absolute tatters. Brogan had clearly loved her little boy, just as her parents had loved her. Yes, drugs had played their part but what I couldn't stop fixating on was the fact that this was mostly a battle of wills between two stubborn, headstrong people. Which happened all the time, didn't it? It was just part of family life. So for me, the biggest tragedy was that fate might have intervened again another way, and it might have only been a matter of weeks or months before the dynamic shifted and the family reconciled again. It could have been as simple as someone seeing through Brogan's carefully constructed mask, or an intervention from Ethan's nursery, or her mum pushing harder. There were myriad ways that the situation could have been turned around, and things for Brogan and Ethan could have been set back on track again.

I said as much to Christine when I finally spoke, and she shook her head sadly. 'If ifs and ands were pots and pans, right?' she said, quoting an old saying I'd heard many times from my own mother.

'There'd be no work for tinkers' hands,' I finished. 'I know that, I do, and I bet many a mother or father has had to concede that their child did what they did, and that wishing there'd been a different outcome doesn't change anything. It's just so bloody sad. And you got all of this from the grandparents, then?'

Christine nodded. 'I did, mostly from Mrs Baines, obviously. There was no holding back with her. I think she's been a long time doing that. I think – hope – she found it cathartic to talk to me. To share things she's probably barely allowed herself to acknowledge, let alone laid bare, particularly to a stranger.' Christine grimaced then. 'I hate to say it, but I think on that front we've been particularly lucky. I feel bad putting it like this, and I'm a little shocked that Ethan's gran was so upfront with it, but Mr Baines's guilt is a huge part of this. He feels dreadful that he stopped her stepping in so many times; that he misjudged how strong his daughter's will would be. He's clearly not a well man, and we really mustn't underestimate what a massive job it will be to take on – to take in – a five-year-old. *Massive*. But despite that, he's really driving things – it's not us, we're not putting them under any pressure whatsoever to be assessed as connected foster carers. It's all him. He's the one really pushing for it now.'

The kettle had boiled by now, and as I stood up to make some more coffee (and tea, of course) I let that piece of welcome news sink in. Connected foster carers were family members or family friends who would step in to foster a child they knew, long-term. The application process wasn't nearly as long as it usually was, and, for obvious reasons, a good deal less stringent. It also didn't need to include the annual training sessions that traditional foster carers had to commit to, as these carers weren't fostering in the same way that we were, but stepping up for just a specific child or siblings. This could be a good thing indeed, especially for Ethan. No, he probably didn't really remember his grandparents, and what he did know about them was likely to be – from what I'd heard and seen – mostly unfavourable. But that was a hurdle, no more than that, especially at Ethan's young age. Yes, he might have picked up the negativity, and maybe seen photographs, but what he *wouldn't* remember was what it felt like to be hugged and loved by them. The chance for them to do that, for him to *feel* that … well, the power of love and hugs was never to be underestimated. And there were no better people than them, hopefully supported by Ethan's father, to raise their little grandson, while – equally important – keeping his mother's memory alive. While he didn't need to know the details of what led to her tragic death at this stage, he *did* need to know how much she'd loved him, and was loved herself, and that never in a million years did she mean to leave him.

'I can see your mind ticking over, Casey,' Christine said, grinning as I handed her another mug of her awful brew, 'and, like me, you're probably realising that this could actually be a relatively short placement.'

'I am,' I admitted. 'And it's all really encouraging to hear. But then that throws up a few more worries, to be honest. I mean, yes, I'm obviously happy that Ethan might soon be back with family, of course I am, but do you think you could give Lydia a nudge re that school place? It's not good for him being at home stuck with just me all day. Not just educationally, but emotionally and socially. He needs that routine, that stimulation, and to be around other children. Have you heard any more about that?'

'Not yet,' Christine said, 'but I'll get on to it right away. Though to be fair, Lydia's been hijacked to deal with a big child abuse case. Multiple kids to be placed, multiple perpetrators to be investigated – and all family members.' She shuddered, then shook her head. 'But we don't want to dwell on that, do we? I'll make sure all this is prioritised and that someone's on to it. Ditto that first contact visit with Ethan's grandmother – and just his grandmother for the first one, as I think Lydia might have told you. Mr Baines thinks it might be a bit much for Ethan to have to deal with them both at first, especially with emotions running high, and him with his foot off. His wife didn't say as much, but I think Mr Baines wants her to prepare the ground for him a little. Keen as he is to do right by Ethan – and be the grandfather he knows his daughter would want him to be now – I'm not sure it's going to come that naturally. Still, that's not for you to worry about. He says he's keen to take the boy on, and we'll move heaven and earth, trust me, to make it work. In the meantime,' she said, downing her remaining tea in two gulps, 'I must be off so you can make the most of your free day. Now, put everything I've told you right out of your mind. Okay?'

To which of course I said yes, but it was hard. Try as I might to concentrate on the positive news about Ethan's grandparents, Brogan's terrible story kept dominating my thoughts, and dragging them downward, as any tragic, senseless death can't help but do.

What I needed, I decided, was a dose of good cheer, via the tonic of speaking to my own children.

So, first of all I phoned Tyler and Naomi to have a nice chat with them on FaceTime, on the one day in the week when I was fairly sure neither of them would be working. The Christmas wedding was, of course, our first subject of choice, Naomi keen to tell me all about the new outfit she'd recently ordered for the occasion.

'You're going to love it, Casey!' she said. 'It's really classy – silver grey, very fitted, with this cropped matching jacket. It's nothing like anything I've ever worn before, obviously. But it's sooo nice. It is, isn't it, Ty?'

'So nice,' Ty said, admirably feigning great enthusiasm, but I could tell he was already bored by the whole subject, bless him. '*So* nice,' he added, with a wink and a grin, which earned him a poke – a very playful and loving poke. Which couldn't help but fill up my emotional tanks again; there is nothing quite like seeing your kids happy in their relationships to instantly give a boost your own happiness levels.

'Ignore him,' Naomi said, giggling. 'Oh, but he did remind me this morning that it's yours and baby Carter's birthdays coming up very soon. Any big plans? Tyler said you're a big fan of parties.'

I Want My Daddy

My son grinned again, and I was touched that they'd discussed it. But, in reality, I'd given mine very little thought. I was going with the flow this year; and not just because Ty and Naomi might not be free. Everyone in the family seemed to have such busy diaries these days. With growing kids of their own now, mine were getting ever busier. There was hardly a weekend that didn't involve military-style operations, both with training and their various leisure activities, swimming lessons and so on, particularly in Riley's case, playing chauffeur and hotelier, as my grandchildren's blossoming social lives dictated.

'I don't know if it's an age thing,' I said, laughing, after admitting I had barely even thought about it. 'Although, to be honest, now we have Ethan, and given how he came into care, I'm not sure a big, family party is the way to go this year, anyway. I just think it would be too much for him. Too soon, too distressing.'

Both Naomi and Tyler nodded. 'But, Mum, you've got to do *something*,' he said. 'Even just a meal out.'

'Oh, that's probably what we will do,' I said. 'And we'll possibly take Ethan with us. And if you're free ...'

'Not this month, sorry,' Ty said, shaking his head. 'I'm mad busy at work and Naomi has another assignment to finish –'

'Which is doing my *head* in,' she added, with feeling.

'But we were thinking perhaps next month?' Ty said, 'We could come down for a weekend? And stay at our

Kieron's, since, you know, you've got Ethan. Plus, there's wedding stuff we need to go through. But we could do a meal out with you and Dad, if that's okay? I mean, we'll still send your presents,' he added. 'You just won't be graced with our fabulousness, I'm afraid.'

'How will we *ever* manage to cope without your fabulousness?' I asked. I laughed, but a great rush of sadness came over me. So silly, because I really *hadn't* thought about my birthday, much less expected the pair of them to come rushing home. I gave myself a mental talking to: must buck up. 'Really, don't worry, sweetheart. Your work and studies must come first. I totally understand, and next month will be lovely; I'll pretend I'm royalty, and have an "official" birthday too.'

Which was the right note to end on, or at least to move on from, and I spent another twenty minutes hearing all about everything: their work, Naomi's training, all the places they'd been to, how they'd already made a couple of really nice friends. By the time we were done, my mental sun had come out, and, as if on stand-by, the actual sun had as well. The leaves were just turning, and the light was softly golden, so, after an hour of frenzied cleaning, and ironing a week's worth of Mike's work shirts, I jumped into the car and headed off to visit Riley.

Unusually, David, her partner, was home too, as well as their two younger kids, Jackson and Marley Mae, and within minutes I had a fresh coffee in my hand, and my seven-year-old granddaughter on my lap.

'I tell you what we could do, Mum,' Riley said, when the subject of my partyless birthday came up a second time. 'I mean, I'm not sure if our Kieron has planned anything for little Carter yet, but assuming they're going to have some sort of toddler-infested house party' – she pulled a face – 'how about we all go out for a nice quiet Sunday lunch somewhere, to coincide with the little lad's next prison visit? That way you need not even mention it to him, and it can't stir up any feelings that would upset him. We could ask Kieron and Lauren if they'd like to come too. I'm sure Lauren's mum would look after their kids.'

So that was that. My birthday would go by largely unnoticed by Ethan, which was what I wanted, and I still had a visit from Tyler and Naomi to look forward to. Life felt suddenly a bit brighter again, the morning's cloud lifted, and, in doing so, made me realise that I'd been a little more affected by the tragedy of Brogan's death than I'd thought. And that, I also realised, *was* an age thing.

I left Riley's at five, feeling tired but rejuvenated, in that way running around the garden with grandchildren tends to do. And my thoughts couldn't help but return to the little boy we were fostering, and how family life was going to pan out for *him*. It was all looking hopeful. No doubt about that. But there was no way of knowing how things would pan out in reality. Would the Baines bond with their grandson? Would they be able to cope with the demands of a five-year-old? Would they have the required energy? They were in their late fifties, and him with ill health, after all. So, it definitely wasn't a given. Especially with the challenge of this particular grandson, who was already showing signs of presenting multiple challenges, even *before* his mother's awful death. And what about this dad of his, and all *his* good intentions? Translating wishes into actuality surely wouldn't be that easy, even with the best will in the world. He was in prison, and even when released would have many challenges of his own to face. Not least in finding a job, and a home. There were rather a lot of ducks to be lined up in a row. So I definitely wouldn't be counting any chickens.

Another random thought had also been bothering me about Ethan. He was only five, so, just like the date of my birthday would mean nothing to him, I imagined that the date of his own mother's birthday, and indeed the date she died, would mean nothing to him either, not for a good many years, anyway. It was just all so bloody sad.

As I waved from my car, the happy contrast of Marley Mae hopping from foot to foot on the doorstep, waving back with a sparkly wand she'd been given at a friend's recent party wasn't lost on me. It had shiny ribbons hanging from it, which intermittently caught the light, and twinkled in the sunshine as it moved. I could do with one of those, I thought. A magic one.

Chapter 10

There was a hammering on the front door just after 6.00 p.m. Mike had just gone in the shower and I was washing the tea things so I hadn't even heard the car pull up. As soon as I opened it, Ethan flew in, iPad in hand. He didn't stop, just barrelled past me into the kitchen, followed more sedately by a tired-looking Heather. In fact, more than tired-looking. She seemed a bit stressed. So much for my fond imagining that he'd sleep the whole way home.

'Is it six o'clock?' Ethan called back to me, 'Is it? *Is* it? *Exactly*?' He too was looking agitated, pumped up with anger, and stabbing his finger towards the oversized clock we'd bought to fill the huge expanse of empty wall. (Open-plan, we'd begun to realise, meant scaling everything up, as our modestly sized stuff looked wrong in such a huge space.)

I followed him through and glanced up at the clock myself. 'Not far off, sweetheart,' I said. 'It's almost ten past now.'

Ethan immediately barged back past me and aimed a kick at Heather's shin. 'Fucking liar!' he yelled. 'You said we would be home at six o'clock, and it's not six o'clock! I *told* you!' he added, waggling the tablet at her. 'You're a liar, you are!'

'That's enough, young man,' the poor woman said as she bent down to rub her leg. 'Remember what we said in the car? That if you didn't stop hurting me, I might not be able to take you anymore? It would be someone else then, wouldn't it? And you don't want that, do you?' She paused. He just glared at her. 'Well, *do* you?'

Heather looked at me then. 'I've had a slap around the head and my hair pulled, I'm afraid, Casey. We've spoken about it before, about how I can't give Ethan an exact time. How I am not in charge of either the traffic *or* the traffic lights, but yet again …' She shook her head and, with Ethan's eyes on me now, rolled her own.

Ethan was staring at me defiantly, presumably waiting for my reaction, the iPad – its timer clearly the cause of our current woes – held tightly in his arms, against his chest. He was ready for a fight – that much was all too obvious. But now was not the time. Seeing his dad again, and for the first time in quite a few weeks now, and with memories about the night his mum had died no doubt resurfacing as a consequence, his emotions would naturally have been all over the place. And as he didn't have the capacity to control them, it was up to me.

'I'm so sorry,' I said to Heather, trying to transmit my feelings to her. 'Sounds like it wasn't the best journey.'

I Want My Daddy

I then turned my attention to the coiled spring that was Ethan. 'You must be very tired after such a long day,' I said levelly. 'I've put a sandwich and some orange juice over on the coffee table for you. *Paw Patrol* is all set up too. You just have to press play. So off you go now, while I see Heather out.'

Ethan hesitated, apparently fazed by the lack of admonishment. He opened his mouth to speak but immediately shut it again, clearly having second thoughts. Deciding upon a scowl, aimed first at me and then at poor Heather, he stomped off towards the living area, where he would hopefully calm down.

I ushered Heather back into the hall, out of earshot. I didn't waste time discussing when and how I'd admonish him. As an experienced family support worker, I hoped, and also assumed, she knew I would do it when I felt the time was right. 'So how did it go?' I asked instead.

'Well,' she said. 'Or as well as these things *can* go, at any rate.' She rolled her eyes again. 'Dad always swears like the proverbial trooper, so it's no wonder the lad comes out with all that bad language. But, yes, I think they were glad to see one another again.'

'Did they talk about Mum at all?'

'Only fleetingly. Well, as far as I could tell. I try to sit a little way away, to give them some privacy, but I do try to listen, and I always take notes. I'll be writing them up later for his social worker. I'm sure she'll send you a copy if there's anything you need to know.'

This immediately riled me. *Well, of course I need to know, you silly woman!* I thought irritably. I didn't say it out loud, of course – just nodded and thanked her. It was clear she was anxious to leave and get home anyway, which made me soften my stance – I mustn't forget that it had been a long day for her too. And, perhaps, I mused, a slightly unsatisfactory one, to boot. She clearly had an ongoing relationship with Ethan, and was performing a vital support role in his life, but it couldn't help but be peripheral – not the kind I'd like at all.

'Do you have far to drive back?' I asked. 'Can I get you a coffee before you go?'

She shook her head, as I'd expected. 'Not too far,' she said, 'and no. Thanks, but I'll probably stop off at a drive-through.'

'So, same time two weeks today?' I asked, as I opened the front door. 'Or were you serious about someone else taking him?'

'Oh, it'll be me,' she said, with the first trace of a weary smile. 'Which is fine. Though I've been asking for the last six months for an escort, to help control him, but no – as you can imagine, no funding for such luxuries. I mean, when he's good, he's lovely, and on the way there he usually is. And the visits *do* go well. There's a genuine bond between them, but –' She sighed. 'I really don't know what it is, but when he gets like that ... well, the journeys back are often horrendous. Still,' she finished, with a wider smile, a knowing smile, one of camaraderie, ''tis what it is, eh? In our line of work ...'

Having waved her off, I closed the door, and wandered back towards the living room. I did feel for her. It was hard enough for me, when I just took him out for an hour or two, and I knew what it looked like when Ethan 'got like that', but at the same time, she did this kind of thing all day, every day. Surely she had been up against worse cases, supported much more challenging children? He was only five, and a young five, after all. Then again, there was no excuse for what he'd said and done and as establishing those disciplinary boundaries was a key part of *my* role, I would have to address it, no question. And, given his age, do it sooner rather than later. But first I had to try to get him to talk about his day. *Fingers crossed*, I told myself as I joined him on the sofa.

'Wow! You must have been hungry,' I said, noticing the empty plate. 'Do you want anything else to eat?'

Ethan shook his head, his eyes still firmly fixed on the TV, while the iPad, I noticed, was still chattering away to itself. 'No, thanks,' he said, as I reached across and turned it off. 'Daddy got me a McDonald's.'

I gaped at him. A McDonald's? In *prison*? I wasn't sure that was possible, but still, the world had moved on in the last few years, and once I thought about it, I did recall someone saying to me recently that in some prisons, at least for some categories of prisoner, food could be, and was, ordered in. Still, it brought me up short, the idea of all the inmates and their visitors sitting round their little tables, cartons everywhere, eating takeaways.

'That sounds nice. So, did you have a nice time with Daddy?' I asked him. 'Did you give him the picture you made for him?'

Ethan finally turned to me, but only very grudgingly, and for a moment I considered turning the television off. Modern life, eh?, I thought, where screens had become demi-gods. And woe betide anyone who interrupted them once in flow. I decided otherwise, however. There was little to be gained in pushing things.

'He said it was cool,' Ethan said. 'He wants me to do him one of the seaside. He misses seeing the seaside, being banged up the way he is.'

Which brought a smile to my lips. And an idea, as well. Perhaps a trip to the seaside could be something I could do with him. And he could do his drawing there, or at least take some photos. I said as much, but his eyes were already being drawn back towards the TV screen.

'Yeah,' he said, when I suggested it might be something we could do together. Then, surprisingly, 'And Daddy said I mustn't worry about the things of yours I broke, 'cause the social always give you money to get new ones.'

I was brought up short. Where to start with such an unexpected statement? Not least how such a pronouncement – and admission from Ethan – might have come about. What things Dad might have asked him about where he was living. I would definitely have to get hold of Heather's notes and delve further.

But this wasn't the time to interrogate him. 'Well,' I

said, choosing my words carefully, 'Daddy's right about that. But, you know, Ethan, it's never good to damage other people's things, even if someone does pay to replace them. You'd be pretty cross if someone stamped on your iPad, don't you think?'

He pulled it towards him. Was he wondering if I was about to do exactly that? 'I wouldn't let no one do that,' he said firmly.

'I'm sure you wouldn't,' I hurried on, keen for the conversation to take a different turn. 'Anyway, I'm very glad to hear you and Daddy had fun. What else did you do? Did you play any games?'

And I genuinely wondered; how was a four-hour prison visit mostly spent? Especially with a five-year-old. They surely didn't spend the whole time sitting chatting. That would be a hard ask of any child. I made another mental note to ask Heather more about it.

'We did play games. Daddy has a big, massive, giant Jenga, only I don't like doing Jenga, so we built London bridges with it and then I knocked it down and Daddy laughed and pretended to be 'noyed at me. And he's going to get giant Jenga when he leaves the big house, too. And he said I can go and live with him when I'm a big boy. Which is next week,' he added, with conviction. He then yawned – he couldn't stop himself – and I could see just how tired he was. Best to leave this, I decided, till tomorrow.

'You *are* going to be a big boy, very soon,' I agreed, reminding myself that the question of where Ethan was going to live, at least as far as *he* knew, was something I needed to bring up with Christine. Because that, I was sure, wasn't an option on the table. Ethan's father still had some months left to serve, and if Ethan had it in mind that he was going to live with him it could well cause problems if and when he was moved on to live with Brogan's parents. 'Anyway, I can hear that Mike's coming down from his shower,' I went on, 'so let's run you a bath and get your pyjamas on for a story and bed.' And now I did turn off the television and he didn't kick up a fuss. Perhaps he was still shocked at his lack of a telling-off, and decided it would be rash to take me on.

In any case, I had already decided to tackle the business of him lashing out at his support worker in the morning. It sounded like he'd had more than enough to think about for one day and he looked shattered. I wasn't surprised when he stood up without argument and made his way up to the bathroom. Despite what he'd done in the car, and the kick-off about the time being wrong (something I needed to log, as it was definitely becoming a theme), he got into bed and snuggled down straight away for his story. And as he yawned through the first part, and his eyes began closing five pages in, he looked more content, I realised, than I'd ever seen him.

Tonight would be a good night, I thought, as I crept out and turned off the lights. Sheer exhaustion, perhaps? Or was it the Dad effect? Either way, it would make a welcome change.

Chapter 11

The next day looked like shaping up to be just as promising as the night before. Ethan had indeed slept well, and, once again all through the night – another whole night without any disturbances. So I woke early, feeling rested and calm and optimistic, and even more so when I looked in on him, while Mike got dressed for work, to find him still sleeping. I loved seeing him like that, in all his tousle-haired innocence – it was good to have that reminder that this challenging child, with all his complicated ways, was no different, in essence, to any other little boy – vulnerable, tossed about on a storm not of his making. And in need of, and deserving, all the love and care and guidance we could give him.

'Someone's in a good mood,' Mike said as he joined me in the kitchen for a coffee before work. 'I don't think I've heard you singing along to your sixties tunes for ages, and getting all the words right as well!'

'Don't be cheeky,' I said, grinning. 'An' don't be bustin' my buzz!'

My little 'Tylerism' had the intended effect. My husband almost choked on his coffee. Which served him right for teasing me, frankly.

'Oh my God, Casey! Just don't, please,' he said when he recovered. 'And don't think I don't know how you suddenly know every song that comes out of that big, grey ball over there. Kieron told me yesterday how he taught you how to create a playlist or something, so that all your awful tunes are handpicked.'

I laughed. He was right. My trusty DAB radio, the one with all the great stations, had been replaced the previous Christmas, courtesy of Kieron and Lauren, with what I considered to be the greatest invention of modern times. The smart speaker. A wonderful device, with a disembodied voice that obeyed my every command. All the kids teased me, including the grandchildren, about how over-enthusiastic I was, speaking to my new friend all the time. 'Alexa, what's the weather going to be like today? Alexa, give me a music quiz. Alexa, tell me a funny joke.' Oh, I was like a woman possessed! And now I'd graduated to more techy stuff, as Mike had noticed, and had indeed created playlists. I now had three; different selections of all my favourite songs, which I would choose between as various moods took me. Currently playing was my 'happy songs' list, which had the added bonus of having the opposite effect on everyone else, so if I put it on, I usually got some peace and quiet.

I Want My Daddy

'You may tease, young man,' I admonished, 'but scientists have proven that starting the day with uplifting music has an effect on how the entire day will go. So you get yourself off to work and leave me to get on with mine.'

I had no idea whatsoever if this was true, but it seemed feasible, so that was good enough for me. And bad enough for Mike that he left half his coffee, and left me with raised eyebrows and a kiss on the cheek.

Ethan must have really needed his shut-eye as it was already past 9 a.m. when Christine phoned, and he was still asleep in bed.

'I've got some fab news, Casey,' she said, 'but first, I've had the report back from Family Support, and apparently Jack Davies has enlisted a solicitor. He has been told the grandparents are being assessed as long-term foster carers for his son, and he has no objection to that. But he wants it filing for court that he wants to play an active role in Ethan's life when he gets released.'

'You must have read my mind,' I said. 'I was going to call you this morning and ask about that. Ethan seems to think he's going to go and live with his daddy. Says he told him he can live with him when he's a big boy. Which he seems to think means sometime next week. I presume Dad is thinking more long-term,' I suggested. 'Which is fine, of course, but if Ethan is expecting that to happen sooner, he'll need putting straight, won't he? Because in his mind, if it's a choice between living with his daddy, who he loves, and his grandparents, who are

111

strangers ... well, that expectation is going to need managing, isn't it?'

'It's already crossed my mind,' Christine said. 'And from the other side, too. The grandparents might well have their own thoughts about that, especially as they feel he's responsible for what happened. In part, at least. So you're right. It's a tricky situation all round.'

'So that's why it has to go to court, then?'

'Well, yes and no. It's also because we haven't had the time yet to make his care plan official, and it will need a judge to do that, especially in preparation for when he leaves you, as it's the court which will ultimately decide Ethan's long-term future. And if Jack *will* be playing a part in that, as he intends to, it all needs to go on the paperwork. And yes, it's also so that if the grandparents do object to it, Dad has the opportunity to fight any decision if he needs to.'

Christine went on to explain that it wouldn't affect anything as far as time-scale went (a court case was inevitable anyway) but if the grandparents had no objections it would make things a lot easier if a judge was the one making all the big decisions, such as when and where any contact would take place, and if there would be a time, for example, when overnights could happen. Jack, as a father who had maintained contact, albeit from prison, actually had more legal rights than the grandparents did, but luckily it seemed he was sensible enough to acknowledge that his son might be better off in a more stable environment than he felt, as things stood, he could provide. Despite what I'd heard about him, I was beginning to respect him.

'And your fab news?' I asked. 'You said you had fab news. Has the contact visit with Gran been confirmed yet?'

Christine chuckled. 'No, not quite yet. But I believe we're almost there. No, I think you're going to like this particular bit of news even more. And if I wasn't holding the phone, I'd be doing a drum roll. Lydia has already found the lad a school place! And better yet – ta da! ta da! – he can start *tomorrow*.'

'Oh wow!' I said. 'That *is* amazing news. Is it our local primary? Oh God, uniform! I think our Riley might have some old stuff saved, and Lauren might have a spare sweatshirt of Dee Dee's she can lend me, but, oh God, I'll have to nip into town just in case she hasn't. Oh and I'll need …'

'Calm down, miss ants in her pants!' Christine interrupted, laughing again. 'The school have said it's absolutely fine if you don't have full uniform, and they can even help out with it – they said there's no point you spending any money when they have piles of stuff that will fit him, including PE kits, book bags and anything else you might need. It's only a temporary placement there, so don't even *think* about taking that bloody credit card of yours out!'

Duly told, I got the name and contact details of Ethan's teacher, then hung up and did a thumbs-up at Alexa. 'Vindicated!' I told her. Casey science was right.

Great music equalled a great day, and it wasn't even half past nine!

Everyone who knows me knows that my day-to-day life is often punctuated with drama; however, this day was already bucking the trend. And it continued to do so. Ethan woke up, twenty minutes later, in a really good mood, and with the autumn sun shining warmly, I made an impromptu decision: to have pancakes, bacon and syrup in the back garden. Yes, it was a little chilly, but we breakfasted (well, more 'brunched') in our dressing gowns, me with my coffee and Ethan still rosy-cheeked from his long sleep. He surprised me by seeming really thrilled about going to school, though it took some explaining about this one being a new one.

'So William and Harlan won't be there?' he asked.

'No, sweetheart, but there'll be lots of new friends for you to make.'

'So Mrs Smith and Mr Graham won't be there either?'

'No, sweetheart, but I know there's lots of other teachers who will be just as nice.'

'Mrs Smith's *not* nice,' he retorted. 'She's a bitch. My mummy said so.'

I caught my breath. Not in reaction to what he'd said. I knew the score there. But because it had been a long time since he'd mentioned his mummy.

'Oh dear … well, no, Mrs Smith won't be there, so you don't have to worry. You're going to love it there, Ethan, but, sweetheart, you know that word you used

114

just now is really not a nice word, and we need to try very hard not to use naughty words, okay?'

He looked up from his plate, one cheek still full of pancake. 'You mean bitch?' I nodded. 'Okay,' he said. 'I won't say that again, promise.'

'Good boy,' I said. 'And one other thing. And I'm not telling you off, but you really can't do things to Heather when she's driving you to Daddy. That's not a nice thing to do, kicking and hair pulling, and so on. Heather is being really kind when she drives you all that way, isn't she? So we need to be kind to her too, okay?'

Ethan continued chewing, then shovelled another forkful into his mouth. Then nodded. '*Okay*,' he said finally.

'So I was also thinking it might be nice to do a picture for her too, before she next takes you to see him. I think it would be a nice way of saying sorry.'

Another nod. 'Heather's got a dog. I'll do a dog for her.'

And that seemed to be that.

Things continued in a similarly calm and positive vein. When we went back upstairs, Ethan allowed me to help dress him without any fuss, and seemed attentive as I showed him how to do things for himself, such as putting on his socks, after I'd turned them half inside out, and managing to carefully feed the tab into the slot in the zip on his hoodie. I had almost no information about how things had been in his last school, but these small acts of independence really mattered.

Ethan also promised he'd be a good boy while we went to visit Riley, to see if she had any bits of uniform we could use. Again, I had already been reassured that the school could help us out there, but if I could kit him out, at least for the most part, before he got there, that sense of already fitting in – and not having to be scrabbling through lost property – would all play its part in reducing the anxiety that any child would feel in his situation.

And he was as good as his word. Somewhat overwhelmed by the larger-than-life personality of my daughter, he became immediately shy and inarticulate. Seeing this, she soon had him out in her conservatory, giving him free rein over the huge array of toys she had out there, some dating right back to my eldest grandson Levi's toddlerhood. With enough space to keep them all, she didn't see much point in clearing out; with young nieces and nephews always round there, and with her still doing a bit of respite fostering herself, Riley's conservatory had become a bit of a toy Mecca.

And Ethan turned out to be a suitably awed pilgrim. He was soon poking into boxes and crates and drawers and baskets, eventually settling down with an enormous bag of pastel-coloured building blocks, ones that used to be Marley Mae's favourites when she was a baby. An odd choice, I thought, but then perhaps he was overwhelmed.

We watched him from the dining room, where Riley had assembled various boxes and bin liners of old clothes.

'Bless him,' Riley said. 'He's small for his age, isn't he? And I *know* you're going to roll your eyes and tell me he's another of your tiny tearaways, but he's so sweet! I hope they're kind to him. It'll be so overwhelming. Big school's overwhelming enough, isn't it, without the added stress of not knowing a single soul there and having just lost your mum? You just want to wrap him up in a snuggly blanket and make it all better.' She grinned across the table at me. 'And yes, I *do* know it's way not as simple as that. Aha – this'll fit him … And this probably will too. So, anyway, what is happening? D'you think the grandparents will come good?'

I filled Riley in on things as far as I was able, as we amassed a small pile of suitable uniform, most of it old stuff of Marley Mae's. There were some of Levi and Jackson's old school trousers in among it all, but we agreed they were a little too far down the one-way street that always ended up at the place called 'cleaning rags'. But that was fine. We managed to find sufficient jumpers and polo tops, all bearing the school logo, that, teamed with the black joggers and trainers Ethan already had, would mean he'd be able to blend in immediately. And as Riley also had a book bag and a *Paw Patrol* lunchbox, I could just pick up some trousers and PE kit from lost property in a day or two.

'So d'you think the grandparents will be up to it?' Riley asked. 'As in reality?'

'I have no idea,' I said. 'I haven't even met them. I mean, they're keen at least, so that's good.'

Riley still looked sceptical. 'Yeah, but not everyone who's your age has your manic levels of energy. They might *think* they are up to it, but when it actually comes to it ...' She shrugged. And then started to tell me about a forty-something couple she'd heard about via a friend, who'd finally managed to adopt, after several failed rounds of IVF, and who, after only three months of looking after four- and six-year-old brothers, had decided they weren't up to it, and the adoption had failed, meaning the boys, highly distressed, went back into care.

'A horrible, just *horrible*, situation, for everyone,' Riley finished. 'Their marriage is in a mess now, as well.'

It was a story I'd heard too many times over the years, and on the increase, as there were fewer and fewer babies up for adoption, and older children – often troubled, often challenging – were adopted instead. And those adoptions *were* challenging, even with the best will in the world. It was no wonder they were at such high risk of failing.

I looked over at Ethan who, apparently oblivious, was busy stacking the blocks up, then, when they were high enough, playing God, and, with typical toddler-type glee, knocking them back down. And then starting the process all over again.

'Aren't you just the little ray of sunshine?' I admonished my daughter. 'There's blood – DNA – on his side, don't forget. That means a lot. They're his grandparents. That *has* to count for something, doesn't it? Plus, social services will support them in every way they can. And if his dad is as committed as he seems to be, that's got to be another positive, even if he is in prison.'

'Assuming, once he's out, he manages to *stay* out,' she remarked dryly. 'Oh, looky here!' she said, holding up a sweatshirt towards the conservatory. 'Ethan, would you like this? Look – it has Chase on the front! And a little bird told me he's your favourite, favourite hero.'

Ethan looked up at her shyly. 'I can *have* that?'

'Absolutely you can have it.' She threw it across to him. And it just brushed the tower of bricks he'd just carefully rebuilt. Which wobbled and teetered, but didn't fall down. And wouldn't. Not until *he* chose to make them.

But Ethan wasn't God. His life was out of his control. I could only hope that he'd be so lucky.

Chapter 12

It felt good to wake up the following morning and know that as of now we were to have a school routine. A regular getting up time, the morning rituals to settle into, the prospect of Ethan spending time with other children and our family bubble giving way to something bigger.

Well, as long as things went well and they were happy to keep him, and I knew I shouldn't get my hopes up about that. Though things were definitely improving in terms of Ethan's general demeanour, it was challenging for any little one to face a new school and all those strangers, and, for a child in Ethan's situation, even more so.

Happily, Ethan seemed to be just as excited as I was, and definitely up for embarking on this new adventure.

'I never wore a "nuniform" before,' he said as he inspected himself in the long bathroom mirror. He glanced up at me. 'Do I look like a man?'

I couldn't help but laugh at the oddness of the question. 'Yes, like a young man, and a very smart young man, too,' I assured him. 'Now come on, let's go downstairs and get you some cereal, because we have to set off in half an hour.'

Ethan's brow creased in thought. 'How many minutes is half an hour?' he asked as we set off across the landing. 'Because I need to get my iPad and set the timer.'

Great, I thought as he scooted off into his bedroom to fetch it. Now I'd have to be sure to be ready myself the instant that bloody buzzer thing went off. I made yet another mental note, to stop putting precise times on everything. Well, at least to try, because it was such an unthinking part of conversations. I'll be there in five minutes. I'll be ready in fifteen. I'll be done in an hour or so. And so on. I didn't know where Ethan's obsession with punctuality had come from, but I had at least now done some bits and bobs of research. And what I'd established was that it was a recognised phenomenon. It seemed that for some children who'd lived in a disordered environment, forcing strict time-scales on things was their way of creating order, and at least having some form of control in their lives. Which all made sense, but I was still searching for other possibilities.

And, in Ethan's case, it wasn't just a question of not being ready, because we were all good to go at 8.25, as it happened, and he insisted we must wait for the alarm before we left.

'We have to *wait*,' Ethan repeated, when I tried to reason with him, explaining that there was no reason, since we were ready to, why we couldn't just leave. 'We can stand by the door and when it's all counted down, I can leave my iPad on the stairs and then we can go. Unless you want me to bring it with us in the car?' he added, hopefully. 'We could guess how many minutes it takes to get us to school then, couldn't we?'

I shook my head. 'Um, no, sweetie,' I told him firmly. 'We'll leave it on the stairs.' For all his sweetness and lack of guile, I hadn't forgotten he had previous. And I really didn't fancy a smack on the head with it if I didn't get the timing on the nail.

'But if we take it,' Ethan began, 'it'll be there for when you collect me, which means –' Happily, however, I was saved by the bell. And, satisfied that we now had permission to leave the house, he didn't object when I took it from him and left it there.

It was only five minutes' drive to the local primary school and, to be perfectly honest, we could have walked there in little more, but I'd decided that, for now at least, we'd go by car. Ostensibly, this was to streamline the process with Ethan. Given our previous outings on foot, this made sense. Less opportunity for him to go rogue on me. In reality, however, it was as much about me being lazy. I was a fair-weather walker, and even a hint of rain or cold had me scuttling to the comfort of my little runaround. Mike thought it was hilarious, ever keen to point out that there would be no time for the heater to warm the car up before I got there, and that by the time I'd found a parking spot even remotely near to school it would have been much quicker to walk in the first place.

He was right on both counts, but I wasn't to be swayed. Particularly not since I'd swapped my old petrol car for electric. I could drive and *still* be green, as I pointed out to him often, batting away all his blather of how much greener I'd be if I 'manned' up and put one foot in front of the other.

Today, at least, I knew I would have no trouble parking; since I had an appointment fixed with Ethan's new headteacher, I was considered privileged enough to drive through the school gates and take one of the coveted visitors' spaces.

It was now that Ethan's nerves began to manifest themselves to me. Getting out of the car, I was surprised at how he immediately reached for my hand, clutching it tightly all the way into school, and through reception, and keeping hold while we waited for Mrs McKendrick, the head, to call us in.

'Don't be nervous, sweetie,' I said quietly, feeling such a pang for his late mother, who would hate, surely *hate*, not to be here with her baby. 'I know it all seems quite scary at the moment, but I promise you that by the end of the day you'll have made some new friends. And I already know all of the teachers here are lovely. They –'

'How?' Ethan said, squeezing my hand tighter. '*How* d'you know?'

'Because my granddaughter goes here as well. She's called Dee Dee. It was her old tablet you borrowed when you first came to us, remember? And –'

But my attempts at distraction were clearly of no interest. 'Do you know which one is going to sit with me at dinner time?'

'Dinner time?'

'To be my dinner mate. So's I'm not all on my own.'

I was confused by what he meant. 'Why would you be on your own, love?'

'Cos at my old school I wasn't allowed to sit with the other kids.'

My heart sank. Nobody had told me about this and I wondered what exactly he'd done to warrant such a thing – it felt so extreme for a child still so young. I'd have to phone Christine when I got home to check it out. I also realised I knew nothing of what this school knew about him. *Something*, I hoped. I dreaded to think of them going in blind. I was confident they would know the bare facts of Ethan's situation because Lydia would surely have briefed them. But did they know enough about his sometimes challenging behaviours, or how best to deal with him if he became angry or distressed? After that first visit, Lydia hadn't yet been back to see him, so it wasn't as if she'd really got to know him. Plus my hunch was that, knowing how much he needed a school place, she'd have been keen to paint him in the best possible light. I squeezed his hand back, and pulled him closer to me, placing my other hand over our joined ones. 'You *won't* be sitting on your own, sweetie. That I can promise you. Yes, a teacher might sit with you, because it's your first day, but you'll be with all the other children too, for sure.'

'But what if –' he began. But Mrs McKendrick appeared then, from her office. 'Come in, come in!' she said, her voice welcoming and bright. 'Ethan, isn't it? We're *so* happy to have you join us.'

We did as instructed, following her into her small, light-filled office, where my gaze couldn't help but be drawn all around the space, as every surface, both horizontal and vertical, played host to something created by childish hands. Drawings and paintings, sculptures, random knick-knacks of every kind, plus an array of cards which pointed to a recent birthday. I had only met Mrs McKendrick a couple of times, but knew she was well liked and much respected. My own nerves settled. I would be leaving Ethan in safe and competent hands.

Mrs Hewitt, who was to become Ethan's form teacher, I knew slightly better. She'd been Dee Dee's teacher as well, when she'd started in reception. I knew Kieron and Lauren thought a lot of her.

'Hello, Ethan,' she said, standing up. 'I'm Mrs Hewitt, your new teacher. Are you ready to come on a little tour of the school with me? And to meet your new classmates? They're all dying to say hello to you. And then I'll bring you back,' she added. His hand was still clutched in mine. 'So you can ask Mrs McKendrick any questions you might have. Does that sound okay?'

Apparently. At least he finally relinquished his grip on my hand. And though he looked wary of the one Mrs Hewitt proffered, he did take it, and with one final glance at me, as if to reassure him, meekly allowed himself to be led away.

'So,' said Mrs McKendrick once they'd gone. 'Down to business, eh? The paperwork never seems to end, does it?'

She passed me all the usual consent forms and so on, and took down all the additional information she needed. And she was right. Despite us living in the age of the internet, it really did seem to grow exponentially. She then turned to another file at the side of her desk. 'I have quite a detailed report here from Ethan's last school,' she said, gesturing towards it. 'And there do seem to be a few issues for us to consider.'

I felt both relieved and alarmed in equal measure. Relieved that they did seem to have a decent amount of intel, and alarmed at the words 'to consider'. What was in there?

'But he can still attend here?' I asked. 'I mean, as in there's nothing to preclude you keeping him here as long as he's with us?'

Mrs McKendrick smiled and removed the reading glasses she'd just donned. 'Oh, no, not at all,' she reassured me. 'Ethan has had a lot of assessments – which is a good thing, and will save time for us, as well as any school he might attend in the future, of course – but he does have quite a lot of acronyms that will follow him around. ADD, ADHD, ASPD and BPD. An awful lot for a child of his age.' She frowned. 'I'm sure you feel the same. But it seems that at least someone was trying to get to the bottom of his problems. Problems that clearly long pre-date the sad death of his mother.'

I was listening intently but found myself wishing I'd brought a notebook to write down those acronyms, a couple of which, if I'd heard them right, were unfamiliar to me.

'And what they mean for *us*,' she continued, 'is that we will need to seek funding, so we can provide a one-on-one teaching assistant for him. I know he may not be with us for long, but once that funding is in place it will make it easier to transfer it to the next school he attends, so I will start that process immediately.'

This was good news indeed. I wondered just what exactly was in his file though. It also reminded me to ask about him having to sit apart from the other children for lunch in his previous school.

Mrs McKendrick nodded. She was clearly not surprised. 'He probably did,' she said, nodding. 'And possibly at break times too. However, he is here now, and we'll turn the page and start afresh. He will join all the others for lunch and break, and, at least for now, we'll just have someone keep an eye on things. He's been through so much, bless his heart, but now that he's settled in your expert and loving care, he might be more likely to settle better in school. Let's hope so, eh?'

I Want My Daddy

'LOL, I don't know about expert,' I said. I never could take a compliment. 'But we're doing all we can to try and help him get through it. And he really is a lovely little lad most of the time. It just seems as though he has a lot of challenging learned behaviours, which we're working hard to try and unpick and sort out.'

'Speaking of which,' Mrs McKendrick added, 're his mum and what's happened, Miss Hewitt has had a word with the children in his class. Just reminding them to try and be sensitive to his situation; suggesting they don't speak to Ethan about his mummy unless *he* wants to talk about her, and to be kind, to understand how sad he will be feeling. It's not a failsafe, obviously – not given their age – but hopefully it will make most of them at least stop and think. Ah,' she said, as the door opened, 'your ears must have been burning, Miss Hewitt. I was just telling Mrs Watson how much you are all looking forward to having Ethan join you. So, Ethan, what do you think? Do you like what you've seen?'

Ethan nodded shyly at her. Then turned to me, 'Casey, Casey,' he trilled, 'there is another boy called Ethan! Can you believe it? And we have our own playground and a football field as well. Can you *believe* it?'

I smiled. 'You know what, sweetie, I'm not sure I *can* believe it. But you just told me, so I'm quite sure it's all true. How amazing! And guess what? Mrs McKendrick says you get to eat your lunch with all the other girls and boys, so that's great as well, isn't it?'

Ethan nodded enthusiastically and I couldn't help but notice that that hand that had been so tightly clasped in mine only minutes earlier was now similarly clutching his new teacher's. In fact, such was his excitement that he was all but managing to drag her back out of the door.

My cue to do likewise, perhaps, so I took it. 'Just phone me if there are any problems,' I told Mrs McKendrick as my parting shot, almost as giddy as Ethan as I headed back out of school, to my little car, and, most importantly, the sweet taste of freedom. A whole day ahead of me! Pretty much the first in weeks now. And I didn't intend to waste a single second, starting with stripping all the beds and getting the bedding out on the line, ready to put back, line-dried and fresh, later on.

And as they tend to on such days, the seconds whizzed by. Once I'd dealt with the laundry and done a quick clean, I typed up all my diary sheets for Christine, including the details of today's promising developments. I also googled the pesky acronyms Mrs McKendrick had sprung upon me and discovered that the two I was unsure of, ASPD and BPS, stood for antisocial personality disorder and borderline personality disorder, respectively. And now I knew what they meant, I was as surprised as she'd been that such extreme personality disorders could be attached to such a young child. But they had, so clearly *somebody*, at some point, must have deemed it fitting to attribute such labels to

Ethan. Why? They must have had their reasons, so what were they?

I sent an email to Christine to ask her to look into it for me, clarifying that I could understand the other two (the attention deficit disorder, and the similar one with the hyperactivity thrown in), and asking if she'd look into the origins of the other two. Were they simply a record of tests he had undergone, or were they actually a firm diagnosis?

By the time I'd done everything, and prepped the tacos I'd planned for tea, so that I could quickly whip them up once Mike was home, it was time to set off again to collect Ethan. As there had been no call from school, I could only assume it must have been a good day, at least from their perspective, but would the Ethan I picked up be in the same high spirits as he'd been when I'd dropped him off six hours earlier? It seemed too much to hope for, but when I got there it was obvious from his body language that he was still in a happy place. He jumped up and down when he spotted me, and pointed me out to his teacher, so she could allow him to run across and meet me.

And he was so full of fizz that I thought he might pop. 'Ethan Franks is my very bestest friend in the *world*,' he trilled, 'and Charlie Johnson is my second best, but he'll be my bestest tomorrow, and Ethan Franks can wait for the next day.'

Though mindful of those acronyms, I couldn't help but smile. 'Wow! Lucky boys then,' I said.

'And how about you? I take it you enjoyed your first day then?'

Ethan slipped his hand into mine as though it were the most natural thing in the world, and for the first time since he'd joined us, I felt a pang of sadness that this would likely be such a short placement. What Ethan mostly needed now was loving and nurturing, and a part of me couldn't help but relish the chance to do just that for him. But the bigger part knew that the best thing of all would be that his grandparents were the ones who would rise to that challenge, welcome him with open arms, open minds and loving hearts, and provide him with that most basic of human needs.

In the meantime, my little livewire continued fizzing through teatime, and for a good hour afterwards as well, regaling Mike with all his tales from his first day, before announcing, at around six thirty, that he was 'tired as an elephant', which made little sense, but, even so, I knew exactly what he meant. And after the quickest bath in history he was in bed, and fast falling asleep, by seven.

Which didn't surprise me. Early starts and a full day at school – let alone a first day at school – took it out on the most robust of children, and I was happy to learn that Ethan was no different. As I ruffled his hair to say goodnight I whispered how proud I was that he'd been such a good boy at school, and that he could do it all over again tomorrow. Then I went back downstairs to Mike to tell him that I actually dared to hope that this school could be just the thing to help Ethan get over his terrible past and settle down.

'You know,' I finished, climbing onto a bar stool to drink the coffee he'd just made me. 'I have a good feeling about this. I really believe we might have turned a corner.'

'Let's hope so,' he said. 'But let's see round it first. Corners have a habit of hiding nasty surprises, and, given the amount of chilli you put in those tacos, that "good feeling" of yours could well just be indigestion.'

He's such a wag, Mike. Or, at least, he likes to think he is. I could only hope that, also, he was wrong …

Chapter 13

Day two of Ethan's school routine started equally well. He woke up and came downstairs as I was drinking my sneaky coffee. I always called this first cup my 'sneaky' one when we had a child or children in because, whenever possible, I'd set my alarm half an hour early, or have Mike wake me up when he was off to work, so I could be sure to be up before they were. That way I usually had the time to have my caffeine fix in peace, which always set me up for the day.

But I didn't mind being interrupted. Ethan just looked so huggable. In pyjamas still, bleary-eyed, curls every which way. I should probably, I thought, take him on a visit to the hairdresser. But not just yet. I had too much of a soft spot for tousle-haired children.

'Alright, sweetie?' I asked him, sliding down off my bar stool. 'Did you sleep well?'

'I think so,' he said, after considering for a moment. Then, reaching for the iPad which had spent the night on its charger, 'Casey, how many minutes till it's school time?'

Of course. I smiled at him and looked over at the clock. I was beginning, now, to get a sense of how this whole thing worked. Where initially I'd been amazed at his apparent grasp of time and numbers (few children of his age could usually count much beyond twenty), I now realised he hadn't yet mastered the clock. He'd just learned to work with tens on his iPad timer. He knew sixty well – he knew if someone said a minute, it meant sixty seconds. And that two minutes was essentially just sixty seconds twice, which he also knew meant scrolling up to 120. He was also clear in his demands involving higher numbers of minutes, which, unless I or someone else helped him, needed to be in increments of ten. Then, once he'd set that, woe betide you if you tried to deviate. It didn't matter that he was yet to be able to tell the actual time, because it was the timer itself that was king.

I decided to try to be clever for once. 'Hmm. Let me see,' I said. 'We need to leave in between sixty and seventy minutes. So why don't you set your timer for seventy, but then, after it gets to sixty, we can set off any time after that?'

Ethan looked at me as though I'd spoken in a foreign language. 'That won't work!' he said. 'Just gimme a number. I need one number. Not two.'

I wondered once again where this bloody obsession had started, and why. 'Okay, sixty minutes then,' I conceded. 'But you know, Ethan, real life doesn't always work that way, sweetheart. Sometimes we can't stick to a definite, planned time. Things change. You might, say, forget to pick up your lunchbox, or need a wee. Or the phone or the doorbell might ring. That's why we make allowances. For all the things that we can't plan. That's why we say things like "I'll be ten *or fifteen* minutes". Or "I'll be there in an hour *or so*". Do you get that?'

What was I thinking? Of course he didn't get that. He was only five years old, bereft and all adrift, and needed every single thing to be just so. The things he thought he could control anyway. 'Six, zero,' he said, scrolling and completely ignoring me. 'That's what sixty is. It's a six and a zero.' Satisfied he'd set it, he flipped the cover closed on the iPad. Then looked up at me, with a butter-wouldn't-melt smile. 'I best get my breakfast now, huh?'

'You best had,' I agreed, picking up the box of Coco Pops Ethan was now pointing at. I poured them into a bowl and went to get the milk out of the fridge, as he sat himself down at the table, the iPad once again open for business.

My kids' generation seemed to be permanently welded to their phones. Ethan was too young for that yet – well, unless it was an old offline one – but if there was one thing that was abundantly clear now it was that his was the age of the all-singing, all-dancing tablet. Little kids seemed to carry them around everywhere, like favourite cuddly toys. Unlike the television – that go-to electronic child minder of my own youth – they could take them virtually anywhere.

By the time I placed the cereal in front of him Ethan had already navigated himself to the screen he'd been after, then launched into the same song he did almost every morning: 'Paw Patrol, Paw Patrol, whenever you're in trouble!'

It never ceased to amaze me these days how such young children, some who could barely string a sentence together, were so adept at controlling all this tech, as well. It was remarkable, really; almost as if they'd been born with a gift. And a gift I definitely did not possess. Like many others like me – of similar age and similarly technically challenged – I could happily tear out my hair when the latest update to whichever phone I had came around. Or at least I would, if it wasn't for my own children stepping in and helping. And this next generation – the likes of Ethan – would be even more tech-savvy. They would have never known a life without it, after all.

Which was nothing to do with gifts, I knew. Just the life they were born into. Sailing into a future that, for them, was completely normal, while oldies like me were constantly having to play catch-up.

Still, that had been the case throughout history, hadn't it? And there was life, and a few basic skills, in the old dog yet. I was therefore smiling from ear to ear precisely fifty-nine minutes later, as I picked up my car keys and waited patiently for Ethan's announcement that we were good to go.

'You're a good girl,' Ethan said as he gently placed his device on the stairs. 'See, you *can* do it.'

My grin faded and became a frown. Was he *playing* me? At his age?

Once in the car, I decided to edge things a little further. This obsession with timings had to have come from somewhere, so where? Had his mum had an issue with timings? Was that it?

'I've been meaning to ask, love,' I said, as we pulled onto the main road. 'You really like sticking to times, don't you? Why is that? Did someone else in your life like to set lots of timers? To be organised, maybe? To make sure they weren't late?'

I was glancing intermittently through the rear-view mirror as I was speaking. He was gazing out of the window, and I wasn't even sure if he was listening. Dare I mention his mum? Perhaps not. Not right now.

'Daddy, perhaps?' I tried. 'Does he like to keep strict times?'

Ethan continued to stare out of the window but after what seemed an eternity, he finally met the reflection of my eyes. He shook his head. 'He's not allowed his own iPad where he lives,' he explained. Then, with a small sigh, 'It's only me. I just like to *know*.' Then he turned his gaze pointedly back to the side window, that particular conversation clearly over.

All conversation, in fact, as the drive was so ridiculously short. Only a couple of minutes later, we'd turned into the school road and he was scanning the pavement, looking out for his new friends.

'Look, Casey! There's my best friend! There's Charlie!' He began waving frantically. 'Charlie! I'm here!' he yelled, even though the boy couldn't have heard him, and when I opened his door and unbuckled his seatbelt he scrambled out so fast he nearly caught his foot in it and tripped over. 'Charlie!' he called, once I'd untangled him. 'I'm your new friend! I'm Ethan! Can we cross the road, Casey?' he asked me. 'I need you to meet my friend!' He then practically dragged me across the road, in his haste to make introductions, to the amusement of the boy's mother, who kindly waited so we could catch up.

'So *that's* Ethan,' the young woman said, as the boys fell into step ahead of us. 'Charlie talked non-stop about him when I picked him up yesterday. He's just started here, right? Are you new to the area?'

I went immediately into my go-to answer. 'No,' I said, shaking my head. 'I'm a local. I'm a foster carer and Ethan is staying with us for a while. I'm really glad to see he's already making friends.'

When I tell people this, it usually elicits similar responses, and Charlie's mum's one was from the usual toolbox.

'Ah, really? Oh, *bless* his heart,' she said, sighing. 'The poor little thing. And thank *goodness* for people like you. So what's the situation there? Is he – sorry, sorry, *no*,' she said, slapping a hand against her forehead.

'What am I *like*? I shouldn't ask, should I? It's none of my business, and you probably can't say anyway, can you?'

'Well, it's –'

'Sorry, no, of *course* you can't,' she said, before I had a chance to tell her that it wasn't covered by the Official Secrets Act. To perhaps reiterate what I knew the kids had already been told; that Ethan had recently lost his mum. After all, it could only be helpful if she *did* know, especially if her son and Ethan became firm friends. But she was clearly in a rush. 'Anyway,' she added, 'I'd better scoot him in now or I'm going to be late for work. Charlie, come along.' She grabbed his hand. 'Well, like I say, nice to meet you!' she added brightly, and they hurried into school, Ethan – clearly anxious not to lose sight of his new best friend – tugging me along in their wake, all concerns about numbers forgotten.

By the time I got home, I once again had that overriding sense of freedom, but riding on top of *that* was the knowledge that freedom equalled the chance to concentrate on other responsibilities, in this case my parents, who I'd barely seen for more than ten minutes at a stretch since Ethan had come to stay with us. Yes, I called them most days, but that wasn't the same and I knew that, at the very least, they needed a bit of face-to-face chivvying. They were now in their mid-eighties and, with their multiple health issues, I knew they were beginning to get reclusive. Not major health issues yet, thankfully, as Dad's diabetes seemed reasonably well managed, but all the small things added up and I knew there were days when they didn't even venture out of the house, Mum because her problems meant she suffered intermittent vertigo and Dad because there was no persuading her once she'd decided to dig her heels in, and even if he did fancy a slow stroll to the park, he didn't like to leave her on her own.

After a quick tidy-up and another mug of coffee, therefore, I was round theirs and letting myself in by ten.

As I'd half expected, they were sitting at the kitchen table, both still in pyjamas, Dad reading his morning paper and Mum listening to the radio.

'Right, you two,' I said sternly, 'the sun is shining, it's not that cold, and you both need to stretch your legs. How about I help you get dressed, Mum, and pop on a bit of make-up for you, and we all head down to our Donna's for a cuppa and a scone?'

This wasn't an unreasonable request. My sister's tearoom in town was a regular outing, far enough to get that bit of exercise they both so badly needed, but not so far that they wouldn't be able to manage the round trip. Plus, they loved going down to Donna's, being made a fuss of and being in the middle of everything.

Or was I just deploying good old-fashioned wishful thinking? No one likes to accept that their parents are getting old and frail, and in that regard I was no different to anyone else. Plus, their house was, as it always was, like stepping into a sauna. And I was at an age where my body thought it was a sauna in any case.

Dad rolled his eyes. 'You'll be lucky, love,' he said. 'I couldn't even get her out in the back garden yesterday.'

'I am *here*,' Mum barked back at him. 'And I told you, it makes me dizzy.'

'You'd feel less dizzy if you took your pills regularly,' he said, frowning at her and then looking pointedly in my direction.

'And the pair of you might be less inclined to bicker if you left these four walls,' I said. 'And if we have to drive, so be it. At least you'll be out. Come on, Mum, let's get you dressed. I can help –'

'I don't need help. And I don't need telling' – she glared at Dad now, her lips tightening – 'what's good for me, either. I can't help how I feel, and if going out makes me feel worse then I should stay indoors, shouldn't I? How does that not make sense to you?'

She was still glaring at Dad, but I could see I was only fanning the flames further. And I already knew this was a battle I wasn't going to win. It had been like this, at least intermittently, for some months now, and despite regular home visits from both doctors and nurses, with blood tests and full work-ups thrown in for good measure, it seemed that other than their general poor health, the only thing that was making them progressively worse was the fact that they were ageing. There was no magic bullet, just medication to treat their symptoms and, while it worked to an extent, there was no getting away from the fact that they were at an age where wear and tear took its toll.

And today clearly wasn't the day to push things. 'Okay, Mum,' I said, shrugging my jacket off. 'I hear you.' I reached over and felt her mug, which was cool. 'Another cuppa first then?' I suggested. 'And perhaps *then* we'll get going … Or, if you're really not up to it, maybe we can sit and have a natter in the garden while Dad at least goes for a stroll.'

'Don't fuss, love,' Mum said, pushing the mug towards Dad. 'Dad'll put the kettle on. You sit down with me.' She patted the seat cushion of the chair Dad had only just vacated. 'I want to hear all about this new nipper of yours. How's he settled in at school? Did things go okay yesterday?'

For all that Mum didn't much want to get out and about interacting with the world in person these days, she'd always taken a keen interest in the kids we had in, and little Ethan was obviously no exception. And as I kept her up to speed during our regular phone chats, she was already well informed. So while Dad made a pot of tea for them and a coffee for me, I filled her in on the events of the previous day.

'So I'm really hopeful,' I finished, 'that this will prove to be a turning point. It's a start, at least. It'll give him continuity, a routine. Plus a chance, like I said, to make friends, to feel normal. He was *so* excited to meet up with his new best friend this morning. Early days, of course. He still has so much to come to terms with, but at least being back in school will –'

At which moment, my phone screen lit up on the kitchen table. And reading the screen before I could – the phone was facing her – Mum made a loud 'tutting' sound. She nudged it towards me. 'Might have spoken too soon, love.'

Of course, it could have been anyone calling and, even knowing it was the school, it could have been about anything, too. Some secondhand PE kit they'd found. Some missed piece of paperwork. But, no, of course it wasn't. Mum's sixth sense, always fabled in the family, was right. I had definitely spoken too soon.

It was the school secretary. 'I'm sorry to bother you, Mrs Watson,' she said, 'but there's been an incident with Ethan, and we need you to come down and collect him.'

'Incident? What kind of incident?' I asked. 'Is Ethan okay?'

'Ethan's fine. He's upset, but he's not hurt or anything.' She paused slightly. 'I'm afraid there was an incident with the class goldfish.'

'Goldfish?' My mind began boggling. What on earth could have happened?

'I'm afraid he's killed two of them. I don't have all the details. Mrs McKendrick will no doubt explain when you get here – he's in with her now. If that's convenient? Are you able to come and get him?'

'Yes, of course,' I said. 'Of course I am. I'll be there as soon as I can.'

145

Both Mum and Dad were looking quizzically at me. '*Goldfish?*' Mum asked.

'*Dead* goldfish,' I corrected. 'Two of them, apparently.'

Dad placed a steaming mug of coffee in front of me. 'What on earth happened?'

'I have no idea,' I said. 'All I know is that he killed them. *Damn* it. And just when I thought things were looking so positive … Anyway, hey ho,' I said, taking my first, and last, sip. 'That'll serve me right, won't it? I'd better head off. And look on the bright side. At least you're off the hook on the nagging front, Mum.'

But she was frowning, shaking her head, and clearly not impressed by my levity. 'It doesn't bode well, does it?' she mused. 'Killing things.' She sighed then. Shook her head. 'Poor little mite. You'd have to be in a pretty bad way to do something like that. Something awful must have happened to that poor child, something *really* awful, for him to even *think* about doing something like that. Killing a defenceless creature. D'you remember that little lad you had that time? The one who killed the rabbit?'

'Accidentally,' I pointed out, as I reached for my jacket.

Was that the case here? I could only hope so.

Chapter 14

By the time I arrived back at school, my head full of anxious questions, Ethan had been spirited away to the library by his teaching assistant, and Mrs McKendrick, who had by now had a proper debrief from both her and Ethan's class teacher, ushered me into her office so she could fill me in before I took Ethan home.

Apparently, he'd been a little 'antsy' right at the start of the first period, after what seemed to have been a slight flare-up with one of the other boys, but nothing they couldn't deal with; they'd just kept a close eye. It was a little after that that the incident happened; it had come about when Mrs Hewitt had stepped outside the door to speak to a colleague, and when the Teaching Assistant, a Miss Peachie, who was busy with another pupil in the book corner, noticed he'd left his table and gone over to the other end of the classroom, and was taking the lid off the fish tank.

'And by the time she got over to him he already had a fish in each hand and was squeezing the life out of them. Literally. And laughing as he did so, apparently – *bizarrely* – which of course caused great distress to all the children nearby. It's obviously a cliché to say no one knows what got into him. But something did, clearly. The question is what? He was plainly in some sort of fugue while he was doing it, because as soon as it was done, he was mortified apparently; dropped the fish, began sobbing and was completely inconsolable. He's alright now,' she quickly added. 'Just shell-shocked by what he did, I think, but, of course, all the other children are still very upset, so we thought it best you take him home, see if you can glean any more from him. Is he under a psychologist as yet?'

I shook my head. 'I wish, but I've yet to hear about when CAMHS is going to get involved. They did say someone called Ian something – Redfearne, something like that? – was going to get in touch – a child psychologist – but I've not had a call or email from anyone yet and I wouldn't be surprised if they'd decided to wait till he's in a more permanent situation before working with him long-term. Different authorities, of course, and what with all the recent cuts, it would be a waste to set up something here if it's just for a short time, and then have to go through the whole process again in a different area.'

'Well, that's no surprise to either of us, is it?' She sighed. 'If I had a pound for every time I've heard the word "cuts" these past couple of years …'

I Want My Daddy

I nodded my agreement. 'So, what has Ethan said?' I wanted to know. 'Has he given you any explanation for his actions?'

'Not really. Not that I'm inclined to believe, anyway. All he came up with was that he wanted to find out what it felt like. To "squish" them were his words. To see how squishy it would feel. He said he didn't mean to hurt them, but, given what the TA said, I doubt that. It's what any child would say, when they're caught red-handed, isn't it? But the TA thinks he did, and I'm inclined to think so too. That something came over him – some great explosion of emotion. What triggered it, I don't know, but something obviously did. Have there been any other similar incidents since he's been with you?'

'Of rages, distress, yes – which was obviously to be expected. But of cruelty, no, never. I mean, we don't have any pets, but, no, this is not like any behaviour we've seen before. So what now? What about tomorrow?' I asked, clinging to hope, but already anticipating the worst.

'I think the best thing is that you keep him at home for the rest of the week. Which I know probably isn't what you want to hear, but I think is what's needed. Give the other children the chance to get over the incident, and you the opportunity to have some talks with Ethan about it, then we'll all have a fresh start next Monday.'

There was no 'if that's okay' or 'if that is going to work for you'. That was what was going to happen, full stop. And I understood, and respected, Mrs McKendrick's decision. There was no way Ethan could return to class tomorrow as if nothing had happened. The fish tank would be sitting there, reminding everyone of what he'd done. Plus, I had a responsibility now to try and coax out what *had* really happened. What *had* triggered such an impulsive and violent act?

'Of course,' I said. 'And if you can put a word in, that would be really, really helpful. I will speak with my supervising social worker, Christine, and ask about some extra support, but Ethan's social worker will contact you directly, I think, so if you could push the urgency for me that would be a big help.'

'I'll definitely do that,' Mrs McKendrick said, smiling at me in that 'I have to get on now' manner that I was so familiar with from my own years working in a school. 'And don't look so worried, Mrs Watson. I think we both knew this would be no walk in the park, didn't we? And I'm sure we'll get there in the end.'

Which was good to hear, definitely. But suddenly a lot less easy to believe.

Ethan's face was drawn and pale when they brought him to me, his cheeks smeared with the tracks of dried tears. He looked the very picture of wretchedness, and fearful now, as well. I didn't doubt for a moment that he now understood the enormity of what he'd done, and, as Mrs McKendrick had said, was mortified.

'C'mon, kiddo, let's get you home,' I said, ushering

him back outside into the car park. I then waited till he was buckled up and I was in the driving seat before venturing a question about what had happened. It was so often the best strategy to avoid face-to-face contact when a child felt in the firing line already.

'Can you explain why you did what you did, love?' I asked him gently as I drove. 'Now you've had a little time, do you think you can tell me?'

I glanced in the rear-view mirror. Unshed tears shone in his eyes. 'I don't know,' he said, his voice barely audible. 'I just … I think I just … wanted to know what it would feel like.'

'To squish them?'

A small nod.

'Even though you knew it would hurt them?'

A single tear slid down his cheek, which he brushed away, sniffing.

'I didn't *mean* to,' he said, crying properly now.

'Okay, love,' I said. 'Okay. It's okay. We'll leave it.'

And we did. There was nothing to be gained by pursuing it. Not while he was in the state he so clearly still was. Instead, I got him in, helped him change and allowed him to snuggle in front of the TV while I typed up my report to send to Christine and his social worker, while it was still fresh in my mind.

I knew the school wanted me to access extra help, but I also knew I'd had to be honest with Mrs McKendrick – social services *were* stretched, and if they could hold off they still would, even with this incident on Ethan's record. It might be 'peaking too soon', would be the bottom line. If they could avoid it, they would not want to waste what could be a one-time opportunity to get a psychologist involved with Ethan now, as it made more sense to do that when he was somewhere longer term, hopefully with his grandparents, where they could use it as an example of how they could be reassured they'd be properly supported.

I did, however, remember a card I might have up my sleeve; I'd called before on the help of an 'in-house' play therapist. Someone trained in psychology (at least our one had been) and who might be able to coax something out of him through play. It certainly couldn't hurt, and I knew I stood a good chance of getting a 'yes' if I requested that, so that's what I included in my long email.

I spoke to Mum and Dad next – I'd already had two missed calls from them – then went out into the back garden to phone Mike, and get him up to speed. He was just as shocked as everyone else had been, obviously, but, not being in Ethan's presence (and seeing a five-year-old in such distress was always going to be upsetting to witness, whatever they'd done), was slightly less inclined to wait before trying to get more from him – was more bullish about *me* being more bullish.

'You know, now *is* the time, love – while it's still fresh in *his* mind. We need to understand what he was think-ing when he did that. And if he really *can't* tell you then he clearly has bigger problems than we first realised.

Don't forget we've had kids in before who hurt animals, and you and I both know that never ends well.'

He was right. Yes, the boy who killed the rabbit *had* done it accidentally. (In fact, as it turned out, his step-father, shamefully, had attempted to pin the blame on him for his own less than fatherly reasons.) But we'd had a number of children over the years who seemed to get pleasure out of harming defenceless animals, and it was almost always reactive, a show of strength on their part, an extreme response to earlier traumas. They'd been hurt horribly themselves, and hurting something that couldn't hurt them back had been their twisted way of trying to gain control. A complicated thought process which often took years to unravel and sort out. We didn't have the time to do this personally with Ethan, but it would be ongoing and somebody would have to, possibly via years of professional help.

There was no getting away from it. I'd been over-optimistic. We had now moved to a more serious place. If he couldn't be in school, it was also a profound backwards step. A horrible situation, and not least for Ethan himself, who would, I knew, be struggling with what he'd done, even if he was too young, and too confused, to make sense of it. Yes, he might have done it while in the grip of rage or distress, but when that moment passed he'd have been all too emotionally present during its aftermath – all too aware of the shock and horror on all his classmates' faces. And that would presumably include his new friends. He was now the boy who killed the fish, and he couldn't undo that. I imagined the breathless recounting to various parents, in various kitchens, that teatime. How was he going to move on from that? And would his class-mates? Was that 'fresh start' on Monday really going to happen?

As for me, all I could do was try to get to the bottom of it, as Mike had said. If I could do that, we could, hopefully, at least try to start processing it.

So I promised I'd try, and as Mike was going to foot-ball that evening, I gave Ethan his tea early, and took him up for his bath immediately after, where I gently probed again while I lathered up his hair.

'Did something happen?' I asked him. 'Just before it all happened? Did one of your friends say something to you that upset you?'

'I wasn't with my friends,' he said 'I was waiting for Miss Peachie.'

'The teaching assistant?' I asked. 'Mrs Hewitt's assistant?'

He nodded. 'I was waiting for my turn to do my writing.'

'So not with Charlie.'

He shook his head again. 'No, I said, I was at the *table*.'

'To do your writing.'

'*Yes*. But Milly was going first.'

'And what were you supposed to be doing, while you waited?'

'Just colouring. But she was *ages*.' I felt him stiffen.
'She said she'd be two minutes. And I *know* that means
counting to sixty two times. And I *know* how to do that
because I'm a clever boy.'

'You are indeed,' I agreed.

But he was getting on a roll now. 'And she called me
clever clogs, which is a bad word, and –'

'Why did she call you clever clogs?'

'When I said I'd already counted and it had already
been two minutes. And she said, "Alright, clever clogs"
and Milly laughed at me when she said that. And so did
the girls on the other table. And she said I had to wait
still and I just got really angry.'

'Because they laughed at you.'

'Because she *made* them laugh at me. I'm not a clever
clogs, I'm *clever*. And then I just got the thunder and
lightning in my tummy, and she shouldn't have *made*
me. And I just couldn't help it. I just … I just … I don't
know why I did that.' He sighed heavily, wretchedly, as
if defeated. 'She should just have come when she *said*.'

I was astonished at his explanation, at his powers of
description, and also strangely lifted by what he'd told
me. *She should just have come when she said.* I was no
psychologist, but to me this didn't sound like a little boy
who would grow up to injure animals. This was an
anxious, angry child who felt he'd been grossly let down.
Who was already struggling with the failure to stick to
promised timings, but who also felt humiliated, belittled,
poked fun at. I held nothing against the TA. How could

she possibly know just how wounding her gentle jibe would be for him? Plus, she was busy, over-stretched, and children had to learn patience. But for Ethan, those two things had unleashed a storm – one I suspected, since he had described it so eloquently, was a feeling, a hopeless rage, that he'd endured many times before.

I had a eureka moment then and, despite my reluctance about ever mentioning his mother, I had to now, because I needed to know if I was right.

'It's okay,' I soothed. 'It's okay, sweetie. I understand. It must be horrible when you get such a storm in your tummy. Here, tip your head back. I'm going to rinse your hair now. There you go. And Ethan,' I said gently, smoothing his hair back from his forehead, 'I understand that it hurts you inside to remember, but did Mummy sometimes tell you she'd only be a few minutes and then she was gone longer?'

A tiny nod again.

'Is that why you learned to set the timer on your iPad?'

I poured another jugful of water over his head while I waited. Then, eventually, 'My mummy teached me. She teached me all my numbers.'

'I see,' I said. 'So that whenever she had to leave you, you knew when she'd come back?'

'When she had to go to next door's. So I could count till she'd be back. So I'd know not to be worried. So I could see when she'd be home.' A silence, much lengthier, ensued.

'And sometimes she didn't come back?' I asked him quietly.

He shot a look at me. A defiant look. As if I'd over-stepped a mark. 'She *always* kissed me better. And she never got cross.'

A *loyal* look, I realised. He was instinctively defending her.

'Why would she be cross?' I asked.

'If I broke things. She never got mad.'

'Broke things because you had thunder and lightning in your tummy?'

He nodded again. 'She didn't shout. She bought me *new* things. She didn't tell me I was a *clever* clogs.'

Which was a lot to take in and lot to digest. But not right then, because now everything seemed to bubble over. With a huge, anguished sob, Ethan began to howl like a baby. He wept and wept as I hauled him, wet and slippery from the bath, and continued to do so as I dried him and dressed him, clinging on to me as if I was a life raft he was terrified of falling off.

And I had nothing to offer but the warmth of my body and the arms that encircled him as he cried himself out. Without either of us mouthing a word of acknowledgement I think we both understood, in our very different ways, that this was the moment when it all became true; that this time it had really hit home that his mother would not be coming back, with her kisses and sorrys and promises of gifts. And if I'd had the power to consign one thing to hell, I thought, that thing, absolutely no question, would be drugs.

It was also, I reflected, as his tears finally stopped, the moment of clarity I had so hoped would come. Once I'd settled him in bed, I told Ethan that he would have a few days off school now, but that everything was going to be alright. I *did* say, because I had to, that I was upset about the goldfish, but that he'd been such a brave boy in telling me all about it, and that I understood and accepted that he was sorry for what he'd done.

I then read him a story – he seemed asleep two pages in, but I finished it – and hurried back downstairs to have a ponder. I was, to use my mother's phrase, like a dog with two tails, and couldn't wait to tell Mike all about it. But first I had to write up another report, a long and full one. For all that it had been school that had brought all this to pass, it hadn't been the turning point: this night had.

Chapter 15

With the whole school thing having unravelled, and the week once again stretching out in such an unedifying manner, I decided some kind of action was required. I was also very conscious that Ethan had reached a milestone in his grieving. What had happened the previous night was evidence – at least to my untutored mind – that he'd come out of that stage of denial.

I had no idea what to expect next but what I did know was that to get out and about felt a much better plan than the pair of us mouldering at home. Plus, there was only so much *Paw Patrol* I felt comfortable allowing Ethan to sit in front of. He needed fresh air and physical activity.

So, my mind turned immediately to what I'd so recently suggested. His daddy had asked him to bring a picture of the seaside when he next came to visit, so what better idea than to take Ethan to the seaside so he could do it while actually there? (Well, if not exactly compose a whole artwork *en plein air*, at least draw it from his actual memories of the seaside, augmented with lots of snaps from my phone.)

Lauren, I knew, was working, but I was pretty sure Riley was free, so while Ethan ate his breakfast, still subdued after all the emotion of the previous night, I called Riley to see if she'd like to join us.

'You must be psychic,' she told me, once I'd run my plan by her. 'I was about to call *you*. I've got Marley Mae home. She's not sick, but she's got bloody nits again. Would you *believe* it? So I've got to keep her home till I've nuked them all or I'll be the most reviled mum in the whole school.'

I could and did believe it. Marley Mae, like her mum, had very thick hair, and – again like her mum, I remembered it all so well – it was a devil of a job to deal with. You could nit-comb for half an hour and just when you thought you'd got them all, up would pop another in the teeth of the nit comb, and not dead, as the packaging always, always promised, but very much alive and dancing a jig. And if you didn't get every last one of the blighters, the whole tedious life cycle would start again.

'Oh, dear,' I said, laughing. 'And duly noted. Cuddles will obviously have to be approached with great caution, but the nits' loss is our gain. Shall we take a picnic?'

'Absolutely not,' my daughter said with feeling. 'Mother, do you not have a calendar? It's late October! I have as much interest in eating sandwiches *al fresco* as flying in the air. Let's do it properly, and have fish and chips.'

Which sounded fine to me. I didn't know if Ethan had ever even been to the seaside, but if we were going, we might as well tick off all the clichés.

The nearest of our favourite seaside places was a sleepy little resort on a pretty wild stretch of coastline, but which definitely still ticked all those touristy boxes. It had the said fish and chip shop, just off the front, a wide sand and shingle beach, with lines of groynes to sit against, and the usual complement of bucket and spade shops. It also had one of those olde worlde amusement arcades, full of quaint retro slot machines and penny falls. They kept a stock of old pennies just for the purpose.

I told Riley I would drive, picking her and Marley Mae up in half an hour, and was really pleased, once I told Ethan our plans, that he was so excited to be going.

'I never, ever been to the seaside,' he told me. 'My daddy says the sea is, like, as big as the *world*, and goes on forever and ever.'

'Well, almost,' I said. 'The world holds a *lot* of water. And it all joins up eventually, at least most of it. So, yes, I suppose it does feel like it goes on forever.'

'We don't have to go in though?' he added anxiously. 'Because sharks and giant stingrays might be in there.'

'We absolutely don't have to go in there. If it was warmer it would have been fun to go paddling in the shallows, but I think you'll be happy enough just playing on the sand.'

'With Marley Mae?'

'With Marley Mae.'

'Like, she'll be my actual friend and play with me?'

I laughed. 'Of *course* she will. You're going to get along famously.'

And they did, from the off, deep in conversation in the back of the car almost as soon as we'd driven off from Riley's. Of course it helped that my eldest grand-daughter is a lot like her mother, never stuck for something to say. She also loved having little ones to cluck and fuss over. It was her very great misfortune (she moaned about this often) that her mum refused to have any more children after her, leaving her with no little sister or brother to look after – she wasn't fussy – and just two smelly older ones to get on her nerves.

Being seven going on seventeen she was also director of operations and Ethan, perhaps gobsmacked at this whirlwind in his midst, seemed more than happy to be directed. So for the first hour, before the fish and chip shop opened, they played a series of complicated games on the upper, shingle beach, most seeming to involve Marley Mae barking out orders and Ethan whooping with joy, doing as directed.

It was after lunch that things took a downward turn. After a fish and chip meal, which was all the better for being eaten accompanied by the smell of ozone and the sound of squabbling seagulls, we bought buckets and spades from one of the shops along the front, and went back down to the beach, where the tide had headed out, exposing a thick stripe of golden wet sand; the perfect type for the making of brilliant sandcastles.

And with a bit of help from Riley, they made a brace of them, complete with moats all around to keep villains out. With the tide still going out they could not wait for the sea to do this so were running up and down repeatedly, filling their buckets, then, as the water soaked back into the sand, having to do it all again.

It was lovely to see and hear Ethan like this. He'd been transported, not just literally, but emotionally. Wrapped up in the moment, and enjoying himself, far away from all thoughts of his troubles. It was also lovely to just sit there with my daughter and chat about the minutiae, the gossip, all the mundane little things, such as what we would buy the kids for Christmas, and how we couldn't wait for the wedding. It was such a nice change from the adult conversations I'd spent the last few weeks having, which had mainly been grim, to say the least. This was exactly what I needed; a day out, cheery chat and watching the children having a ball.

The happiness, however, was short-lived. We'd been on the beach again for just over an hour when we were joined by another family, a big one. And who, inexplicably, given the huge beach was mostly empty, parked themselves only about ten feet away from where we were sitting. I never really understand why some people do that. Is it just that humans unconsciously gravitate to other humans? Which was fine, and is fine, but on that day and in that situation, it couldn't help but change the feel of it all.

This was not least because, as well as Mum and Dad, and presumably Gran and Grandpa, they had three children, all girls, who I guessed were under five. In fact, the littlest didn't look more than eighteen months old. And little by little – Riley and I watched it happen – Ethan, who'd been so wrapped up in their game, became self-conscious and distracted, continually looking across to where they were.

The two older girls, obviously sociable souls, bless them, also seemed keen to get involved. Their own buckets and spades were soon pulled out of the big family beach bag, and though Marley Mae was quick to suggest they made their own extra sandcastles, they seemed keener to join in with the water replenishment, the better to fill both the existing moats.

This continued for some time, and without any problems, but then the mum started producing various picnic items, calling to her little ones to come away.

The older of them, the one we worked out was called Poppy, grabbed Ethan and asked if he'd like to go with her and get a cheese string. He shook his head, and I heard him tell her he wasn't hungry. But she persisted. They apparently had mini-rolls as well. 'And your sister, too,' she said. Like Marley Mae, she was chatty. 'It's fine,' she went on. 'My mum won't mind you sharing. Go on – ask your mum. We're only sat just over there.'

Though I only really picked up half their conversation, the words 'sister' then 'mum' were clearly having an effect.

'That's not my sister,' Ethan told her, the volume of his voice rising. 'And that's not my *mum*. My mum's *dead*! She died and they took her *away*!' He then threw the bucket of water he was holding – not at anyone, thankfully – and ran off, sobbing loudly, towards the water's edge.

I watched the girl's mother's hand fly to her mouth. Then she looked across to us with an expression of apology. 'I am so sorry,' she mouthed, as she got to her feet and headed over. 'So sorry. The poor mite. I don't know what to say.'

'It's okay,' I said as I too got to my feet. 'You weren't to know.' Then I jogged down to the water, some way away now, and with the distance increasing. Ethan was standing there, looking out across the grey, foam-flecked sea. I could see his shoulders shaking.

'Oh, sweetie,' I said when I reached him, crouching down to his level. 'That must have been tough for you. *So* tough.' I took his hands, and he let me. They were wet and very cold. 'Oh, bless you, love,' I said. 'You're freezing. Tell you what, shall we go and get some hot chocolate? With marshmallows in, perhaps? Marley Mae *loves* her marshmallows.'

But Ethan, the tears sill sliding down his cheeks, shook his head. 'I don't want nothing,' he said, not aggressively, just oh so sadly. 'I just want my mummy back. I just want my mummy.' He loosened one hand so he could rub his forearm across his eyes and gulped back more tears. 'I wish my daddy was here.'

'I know, sweetie, I know,' I said, squeezing his hand and coaxing him back up the beach. 'And you'll be seeing him very, very soon now, remember. Just, let me see, four more sleeps. So that's not so long, is it? And in the meantime we'll do him some lovely pictures of the beach, like you promised him, and …'

'*Stupid* beach,' he said. 'I *hate* it here. I just want to go home. I *hate* it,' he said again, then looking across at the now-subdued family, shouted to no one in particular, 'An' I hate *you*!'

We'd returned now to where Riley was gathering all out bits up, while Marley Mae scooted back down to the sea to rinse out the buckets. Riley had caught the tail end of what Ethan had said.

'I agree, Ethan,' she said briskly. 'I hate the beach too now. I've got sand in my pants and I'm getting very cold. So's Marley Mae. Let's head straight home now, shall we?'

Ethan nodded sadly and we walked back to the car in silence. Maybe things like this were too soon, I thought, but when then? There would always be times when he would bump into families, wherever he went. Maybe he had to go through things like this before it all became a bit easier to bear. The truth was, I didn't know. I hadn't experienced a loss like he had, and I'd not looked after other children who shared the horror that he'd endured.

The only positive to hang on to was that Ethan hadn't had a meltdown. He'd felt wretched but hadn't lost control of himself. Yes, he'd shouted his distress, but who would castigate him for that?

Even so, it was a sad end to what had been a lovely day. And there was very little anyone could do to make it less sad. Only time had it in its power to do that.

Chapter 16

Knowing how busy she was, I hated to encroach on Christine's weekends, and especially this week, since I knew she'd already been away at a conference for two nights. But when she phoned me on Friday morning to say we needed to chat about my emails, I put aside my sense of guilt and went for it anyway.

'I hate to ask this,' I said, 'but I don't suppose there's any chance you could call at ours again on Sunday, is there? There's such a lot to talk about and, as you know, I have Ethan at home with me again now until Monday, but there's another prison visit organised this Sunday, to see Dad, so I was thinking, rather than do it on the phone in the evening, that we could perhaps ...'

She didn't even let me finish the sentence. 'For goodness' sake, Casey, stop being so apologetic! Of *course* I can,' she added. 'In fact, I'll be there with bells on. Him indoors is away fishing in Scotland with his mate, so I'm footloose and fancy-free anyway. Well, I say that. I've a whole ton of paperwork to do, but that can wait. Besides, it'll be nice to see you on your birthday. You kept that quiet, didn't you?' She laughed.

I did too. 'I've reached the age where silence is golden. I don't even want to *think* about it, let alone celebrate it. Well, bar lunch with the family, which I *am* looking forward to. But is the morning going to work for you? If you're keen to have a lie-in …'

'Morning's *fine*. Nine o'clock? Actually, what time is Heather Wilkins picking Ethan up? It'll be nice to say hello to him if he's not off too early.'

'Just after nine fifteenish.'

'Then we've a date. I'll bring cake. In the meantime, sending positive vibes in your general direction. Oh, and congrats on the breakthrough. I know the circumstances weren't pretty, but it really does sound from your emails as though he might have turned a corner. How's he been since? Any calmer?'

'Probably not the word I'd have chosen! But better, definitely better. I think we're moving in the right direction.'

'On which positive note, then, I shall bid you farewell. I've a meeting to dash to, and I imagine your hands are full.'

I looked across at where Ethan was building one of his skyscraper towers and, as if on cue, with a grand swipe, he dashed it to the floor, bricks skittering noisily across the laminate. I laughed again, wryly. 'You could say that.'

I Want My Daddy

In fact, after his upset at the beach on the Wednesday, Thursday had been a good day. He'd come supermarket shopping with me and had enjoyed helping me plan the following week's dinners, and in the evening I'd transferred some of our photos to his iPad so he could use them to create some nice pictures for his dad.

But there were hard times ahead of us. He was a child who'd lost his mum. And now he'd finally begun speaking openly about her, I think it really had hit home that she wasn't coming back. And along with that had come periods of a stillness that I'd not seen before. I'd catch him sitting at his iPad but staring into the middle distance, and though it was impossible to guess what thoughts were going through his head, instinct told me she was suddenly at the forefront of his mind, in a way that she'd not been allowed in his headspace up to now. And tragic though it was, this was a key part of his grieving process.

I'd also phoned school and, while he was outside playing in the garden, managed to have a decent chat with Mrs McKendrick. I'd explained what had happened and how timings and punctuality seemed to be triggers for Ethan, and, relieved that we seemed to have found an explanation, she promised to have a word with the relevant staff members so that when he returned they could hopefully avoid any further meltdowns. She also told me that she was happy for him to come back to school the following Monday, especially after I told her that I'd requested some urgent extra support in the way of regular sessions with a play therapist.

But by the time Sunday morning came around I was ready for a break. The unburdening of Ethan, though obviously welcome, seemed also to have unleashed a different beast, and a very lively one, who would randomly appear. Well, perhaps 'beast' was a slight exaggeration, but definitely a rather feral kitten.

It was as if Ethan been holding his real self inside so that he didn't have to reveal anything that might be hurtful to him, but now that he'd let that go, it was as if he was now free to be himself. And 'himself', when he wasn't going through one of his quiet, sad phases, appeared to be quite the wild child. For starters, once he'd regained some emotional equilibrium after the two days of distress, he seemed to have boundless quantities of energy. He no longer walked around the house. Instead, he ran, he hopped, he scampered – jumping up and down from various items of furniture to get where he wanted to go, and no amount of my telling him not to seemed to work. He was constantly 'bored' (no child could have needed to be in school more) but needed lots of extra stimulation to get him interested in something, and by the time Sunday rolled around I was frazzled, feeling all of my fifty-something (as I'd remain till I hit sixty and could be in denial no longer) years.

I had been used to the challenges of this age group for decades; with my own kids, my foster kids and my grandkids as well. But I knew I'd reached that age where that old chestnut about grandkids – 'at least you can hand them back!' – really resonated. I obviously didn't want to 'hand' Ethan back. It was my job to take care of him. But at the same time, he was at an age where he *should* be in school, and I should have that time to recharge my own batteries, while his own batteries ran down over a long busy day there. But there was no such respite while he was off school; I was very much flying this particular mission solo.

So, when Sunday morning dawned, I didn't even *think* about it being my birthday. I was just excited at the thought of Ethan going to see his daddy – almost as much as he was – and of me having a whole day to myself. We were both washed and dressed, and Ethan suited and booted, a good half hour before either Christine or Heather were due – time I managed to coax Ethan into filling productively, finishing off another picture he had already started for his daddy, then colouring in the drawing of a dog I had done for him, the gift he'd promised he'd do for Heather two weeks earlier.

He was just adding the final flourishes in lurid fluorescent felt tip when Christine arrived at the front door.

'Cakes,' she announced, brandishing the small box she had with her. 'Four cakes,' she added, smiling across as Ethan left his drawing. 'One for you, Ethan, and also one for Heather. For the journey. Or is he allowed to have his now, Casey? Perhaps that might be better. That's assuming you like cake, Ethan? Do you?'

'*Yes!* I *love* cake!' Ethan yelled as he ran, arms out behind his back as if they could propel him towards it faster, and leaping straight up onto one of the bar stools as she set the box down. 'And I need to eat mine quick 'cos I'm going to see my daddy soon.'

'You are indeed,' I said, 'so please be careful not to get messy. That's a clean jumper, remember.'

'It's Chase, see,' he said proudly as he stretched the new jumper out so that Christine could admire it. 'It's a new one Riley buyed me. It's a *Paw Patrol* jumper. Off the telly. I've also got *Octonauts*. I weared that one yesterday. Do you like *Octonauts*? My favourite one's Shellington.'

I grinned across at Christine as she handed him a muffin, while doing her best to answer his steady stream of questions. There was no point in my trying to get a word in, so I didn't. Ethan could chatter for England just lately – about anything and everything, hardly pausing to take a breath. It made it difficult to keep up, as he would jump from one subject to another, and I could see Christine was struggling just as much as we did. I think she was as relieved as I was when the door-bell rang again.

'Ah!' I said, just as the last of Ethan's muffin vanished. 'That'll be Heather. Come on, sweetie, let's give your hands a wipe, and don't forget your pictures. And remember what we talked about? About being really, really good for her? No getting angry about times today, okay?'

Ethan nodded solemnly as I held his coat up for him to push his arms through. 'I will, Casey, I swear. I'll be a good boy all day. I won't bop her, I promise. Even if she needs it.'

Christine stifled a guffaw as she de-boxed our own cakes – custard slices – leaving the remaining muffin for Heather to take with her, while I went to the front door to let her in.

'He's full of beans today,' I told her, 'but fingers crossed the right kind of beans, and re this,' I added, as I handed her Ethan's iPad, 'we've had a bit of a revelation as far as timings are concerned, so hopefully you won't have a re-run of last time. Fingers crossed, anyway. Oh, and Ethan has a present for you,' I added, as he joined us and thrust it at her.

'It's a moon dog,' he told her proudly. 'It lives on the moon. And that's laser beams,' he added, pointing to various neon squiggles. 'It can shoot laser beams out of its fur.'

'Well, that's a great skill to have,' Heather said, nodding a hello to Christine. 'To shoot space baddies?'

'Not to *shoot* things. To make things go *sparkly*. You've got a cake too. The lady bought it. But if you're not hungry, I don't mind eating it for you.'

'Well, that's very kind of you,' Heather said. 'And we'll see. Now, then, are you all ready to get going?'

'Wow!' Christine said the moment they'd left. 'I see what you mean about the change in him. He's turned into a bit of a livewire, hasn't he?'

'You could say that,' I agreed as I went across to boil the kettle. 'He has way too much energy to be stuck at home with me, which is why I'm so relieved the school have said they'll have him back. He really needs the stimulation and the company of other children. I just hope we can make it work this time.'

Christine shook her head. 'None of that "hoping" nonsense. We *will* make it work. Not least because your request for a play therapist has been granted, so expect a call early next week to arrange things. She's very flexible too, so if after school is a problem – I know you like to be organised with tea and a bath and bed routine – she said she is happy to work Saturday mornings too, so whatever works best for you. Good news, eh?'

It certainly was. I often thought that fostering children was like putting together the pieces of an intricate puzzle – a bit like doing a jigsaw. When the kids first came to us, it was all about building the outer edges, the framework that held everything else together. We could worry about the internal stuff once all that was done. Then, slowly, we would start to build in towards the centre, linking up the pieces, one by one, from that carefully constructed border. And more often than not, just like a real jigsaw, the very centre pieces were hidden beneath red herrings; ones that looked like they might fit, but, once tested, didn't. And there would always be that one piece, that one elusive piece of puzzle, that you'd have to trawl and trawl and trawl for. Only once *that* was in place would all the other remaining pieces slot in.

I Want My Daddy

It felt a bit like this with Ethan – that now we'd found that one elusive piece, that 'key to Ethan', as I thought of it, from here on in, the rest would be, as Marley Mae would say, 'easy-peasy, lemon squeezy'.

I just prayed I was right. That I had at least found *a* key to Ethan. And though no simple metaphor could ever match the complexity of a traumatised child, I did feel we were making important progress. He would, and must, come to terms with his new situation eventually, but the sooner we could help him onto the road he must now travel, the smoother and less traumatic the journey would be. And a play therapist – another person to assist him with that journey – was going to be a very welcome pair of extra hands.

Once I'd made us drinks, and we'd made inroads into our enormous vanilla slices, we went through the detail of the emails I'd sent Christine, and how we could work with the school to make sure Ethan had all the extra support he might need. We also discussed how I'd probably need some extra support in the unwelcome event of there being further exclusions.

She also informed me that Lydia Heptonstall, Ethan's social worker, had assured her that she would make fortnightly visits going forwards, rather than the statutory six-weekly visits, and would take him for days out as well. That, however, wouldn't start for another two weeks at least.

'Sheer pressure of work, I'm afraid,' Christine said, downing the dregs of her tea. (It never ceased to amaze me how quickly she could polish off thermo-nuclear-heated drinks.) 'But let's not get too doomy and gloomy for I also bring good news about the grandparents, only confirmed by Lydia on Friday afternoon. She's had several meetings with them now, and tells me that they seem genuinely excited about the prospect of having Ethan back in their lives. And yes, you heard correctly. That's a "they" and not a "she" – the grandad is going to be at their first supervised contact visit too now.'

This was good to hear. It would be Lydia's job to get to know the couple well enough that she could present them to her managers as being suitable carers for Ethan, and who, in turn, would present that to the court. And, by the sound of things, this was all going well. 'That's brilliant news,' I agreed. 'Do we have a date set as yet?'

'We do indeed,' Christine said. 'Assuming it works for you, they have pencilled in next Friday, after school. And at *your* local contact centre – so no travelling to worry about either. How's that for a turn of events?'

'It just keeps getting better,' I said, raising my vanilla slice in celebration. 'Here's to it continuing that way.'

'I'll second that,' Christine said, similarly lifting her half-eaten cake.

Christine left after about an hour, having surprised me with a beautiful bouquet of flowers she had stashed in her car, and leaving me plenty of time to get myself titivated and suitably dressed to meet everyone else for my birthday meal. Mike had left the house early to have a fried breakfast with Kieron before going to watch football practice, but he too was back to get ready in good time, and by 1.30 p.m. we were in the car and on our way to the restaurant.

'This will be the quietest birthday I've had for years,' I said to Mike as we drove, 'but it just seems right, you know? Given everything.'

Mike glanced at me and frowned slightly. 'You don't mind, do you?' he asked. 'I mean, genuinely? We could organise something else if you wanted to. I'm sure it's not too late. Well, yes, it's obviously too late to cancel lunch, but I'm sure it's not beyond us to arrange a child minder for Ethan for one night, so you and I can go and hit the town as well.'

I laughed and shook my head. 'Hit the town? No, love, thanks for the offer, but lunch with the kids will do me just fine.'

In truth, I did sometimes miss those spur-of-the-moment nights out, that sense of being young and care-free, and able to 'throw a few shapes', as Tyler would always put it, but when I thought about the next-day hangovers, I was actually quite happy to give them a miss. Besides, running around after a five-year-old meant throwing enough shapes already; my life was quite rowdy enough every day. Plus, what I really craved currently was just some relaxing adult company; to sit round a table with my nearest and dearest, and just to enjoy being with them.

But not, perhaps, expecting quite so many of them. Because the moment I stepped into the restaurant – our small local Italian – I realised that I had been hoodwinked. If it seemed as if the whole restaurant had been taken over by our family, that was because it had. Every face I saw was a familiar and dear one. And just to press the point home, everyone immediately stood up, and performed a cringe-making rendition of 'Happy Birthday'.

And what a din they made too! Which was hardly surprising. As well Kieron and Lauren, Riley and David, and all of the grandchildren, my sister and her husband were there with our niece and nephew, plus two of our closest friends had come too. And Mum and Dad were there, despite all their moans and groans a few days earlier – sneaky so and sos – and even Tyler and Naomi, despite saying they couldn't (even sneakier, in my view), had come over from York.

So not a quiet birthday at all, then. I, of course, cried, then chastised, then had the loveliest afternoon, and by the time we were home, stuffed and tired, I felt not only pleasingly recharged but super-charged, ready to deal with whatever came next. And, better still, with the knowledge that Ethan would be back in school in the morning, where he needed to be.

Even better was the news from Heather that both the visit and, as important, at least from her point of view, the journeys to and from the prison had gone well.

I Want My Daddy

Ethan himself, once Heather had left, was demonstrably shattered, in that way that lengthy car journeys are apt to make you feel. 'Plumb tuckered out,' as Mike quipped when I came down and joined him on the sofa, after the shortest bath–story–sleep routine in history. Though just as I was about to tell him how optimistic I felt about how everything was now going to fall into place, he lifted a hand and said, 'Chickens.'

'What?' I asked, confused.

'And the hatching of,' he added. 'And your tendency to count them too soon.'

'Oh, give over, you bloody pessimist,' I said, throwing a cushion at his head. 'I am fully confident this time. We've got this.'

But, of course, he was right. We had done no such thing. That elusive jigsaw piece? Yes, I held it in my hand, but I was still a way off working out where to place it.

Chapter 17

My husband being right is a constant source of irritation, but, at the same time, it's not altogether unexpected. Where I am, and always have been, an incurable optimist, he has always tended more to realism. Not pessimism; he's not a glass half-empty person. Just a devotee of the principle that if you tread a middle ground you'll, at least most of the time, get no more or no less than you expected.

Which, to my mind, is a good balance to have in a marriage, with his pragmatic world view tempering my frequent flights of fancy, and my default cheeriness meaning we rarely tend towards the gloomy.

The gloom couldn't help but come sweeping on in, though, when, at eleven thirty on Monday morning, my mobile phone rang and I could see it was the school calling.

And straight away, I knew I *had* counted those flipping chickens.

It was the head, Mrs McKendrick, and her opening 'I'm so sorry' told me instantly that my instinct had been correct. 'It's Ethan,' she went on. 'I'm afraid I'm going to have to ask you to come and collect him.'

'What's he done this time?' I asked her. 'Is it a timing thing again?'

Apparently not. It seemed Ethan had been involved in a fight at morning break. Though not one that he'd started. He'd tripped over and cut his knee while playing football and, seeing the blood, he'd become really distressed. He'd started to cry then and, instead of doing anything to help him, two of the boys he'd been playing with started laughing at him. The playtime supervisor, one of the teachers, had heard the commotion and run across, but by the time she'd got to him, Ethan had completely lost the plot, lashing out and violently lunging at the boys, kicking and punching until she managed to pull him off.

The way Mrs McKendrick described it, it sounded like a brawl between teenagers, rather than a scuffle between three five-year-olds. And I sensed then that she could imagine what I was thinking.

'I know what you're going to say,' she went on. 'And no, it *wasn't* Ethan's fault, and the boys *were* rather unkind to him, but these violent meltdowns ...'

'He has a fear of blood. I've not quite worked out where it's come from, but I imagine that'll be why he became so distressed. Which is not to say –'

'I *do* understand,' she interrupted. 'But he clearly has issues around impulse control still, and I think we need to ask you to keep him home until he's at least had a couple of sessions with his therapist. He really does need to learn how to play with others and cope with the kind of structure in place in a school.'

I bit my tongue. There was really no 'I think we need to ask you' about it. It wasn't up for debate. At least, not with me. Ethan was again being suspended. And this time, I felt, rather unjustly. I really wanted to ask if the other boys, the ones whose callous jibes had caused Ethan to react the way he did, would be getting such severe consequences. I didn't though. It wouldn't alter anything, and it wasn't my business. Instead, I grabbed my coat and car keys, drove to school, collected a tearful Ethan and brought him home. It was what it was and there was no point getting cross.

There was every point, however, in maintaining the equivalent of a school routine for him. Indeed if he was going to be at home for any length of time, perhaps I should ask the school if they could email me some work for him to do.

'I'm sorry, Ethan, love,' I said, as I stuck a plaster on his cut knee, 'but there's no iPad and no TV until 3.00 p.m., okay? That's the time you should have been at school till, so until 3.00 p.m., you need to occupy yourself some other way. You can do some pictures, or use your bricks, or play with your toys quietly, but no TV or devices till later. Do you understand that?'

Ethan nodded glumly. 'It's because I was naughty.'

'Not naughty, sweetheart,' I reassured him. 'I know those boys made you upset, and this *isn't* a punishment, but the reason you're not at school now is that you need to learn how to control your temper when someone upsets you, so you don't end up getting *more* upset, or ending up in fights. I understand,' I said, hugging him. 'It's hard trying to settle somewhere new, and to feel comfortable. But we'll get there. You'll see. And in the meantime –'

'But how will I set the time?' he wanted to know now. 'If I can't set it, how can we make the timer go off at three o'clock? Or maybe you can?' he added, having obviously just thought of it.

Despite every fibre telling me I shouldn't, I agreed that I would. We could work on weaning him off his obsession with timings at a later date. For now I was happy that he understood what was happening, and why, so I set the timer and watched him trot off upstairs towards his bedroom.

'I'll build a *Paw Patrol* control tower,' he said, 'I'll use my bricks and my figures.'

I watched him until he got upstairs and then pulled the living-room door to, so I could call Christine. There was at least a slim chance, surely, that the play therapist she'd talked about could come out to us a little sooner than planned. If I was to ever get Ethan back in school and actually keep him there, I needed her as urgently as possible.

Happily, my timing, for once, couldn't have been better.

'Your ears must have been burning,' she said, when I explained the situation. 'I have your play therapist sitting opposite me as I speak,' she went on. 'And we were just this minute looking at her diary for the next fortnight. What are the chances of that, eh?'

Christine went on to explain that Grace, who'd been assigned to us, was a very new appointment, and they'd been sorting out the handover from the outgoing therapist. 'And by the looks of it, tomorrow morning might work – ah, yes, she's nodding – and then, given we don't yet know how long he'll be out of school, we can stick with that weekly gig going forwards. How's that for bloody marvellous?'

I did a Tyler-style fist pump. 'That is beyond bloody marvellous,' I agreed.

Grace herself called me early on the Wednesday morning, both to let me know she'd had a thorough read-through all of Ethan's case notes overnight, and to ask if there were any specific areas of concern that I wanted her to prioritise.

'It's school where the issues mostly lie,' I explained. 'Well, wholly lie, in fact. Getting along with his peers – he already had a patchy attendance record before he came to us, as you'll have noted, and I'm not sure his school experience had been that positive, even before his mother's death. That, and learning to manage his anger. He's fine playing just with me, or on his own. Oh, and he is finally, at least sporadically, talking about his mum now. Mentioning her name, at least, which, to me, has felt like real progress. Though I'm not sure how he'd cope if her name came up in school. Oh, and blood.'

'Blood?'

'He has a fear of it. Seeing it. There's been two incidents now, one with me, one this school incident, where the sight of blood has really distressed him. As far as I know, there was no blood at the scene of Mum's death, so I'm wondering where and why it might have started. Perhaps that's something you could explore with him too?'

'Absolutely. That's exactly what I'm here for,' she said. 'And I should be there within the hour. Well, assuming I don't get lost, that is. I am completely at sea here. And so is my sat nav – it actually took me *to* the sea yesterday, instead of Aldi, as I'd asked it. And if I'm not with you by ten, send out a search party …'

That Grace had the same soft lilting Liverpudlian accent as Christine wasn't a coincidence. It turned out that it had been Christine who had headhunted her to come and join our local authority, when she and her husband had spoken about moving away from the city.

I had already twigged that from our brief chat on the Monday afternoon, hearing her soft Liverpudlian accent down the phone.

I Want My Daddy

'I've known Christine for years,' she told me, as she put down the cabin-bag-sized pull-along suitcase which I presumed held the tools of her trade. 'We worked together as trainees and we've always kept in touch. And then she made me an offer I couldn't refuse. And so far, so good. Ah, and who is this, then?'

Ethan, who'd shyly come up and was peering up at her from around my legs, immediately darted back behind me, out of sight.

It was a shyness that didn't last long though. It wasn't much after ten and he was already getting restless. A new face, and a smiling one, was a welcome distraction.

'This is Grace,' I told him, grasping his hand and coaxing him out in front of me. 'She's come especially to play with you.'

'Indeed I have,' Grace said, squatting down to Ethan's level. 'And I've brought a bag which contains all sorts of fun things to play with. Do you have any special toys you like playing with best?'

'I've got Chase. He's my buddy,' Ethan told her, his shyness abating. 'Shall I go and fetch him down from my bedroom?'

'That would be grand,' Grace replied. 'And I know all about Chase. A little bird already told me you like *Paw Patrol* best of all, so I've brought some special *Paw Patrol* stickers. Though I only give them out to little boys who like to play. Do you want to go and fetch Chase and we'll play together?'

Ethan needed no further encouragement. And I felt

encouraged too. Grace reminded me very much of Christine, and not just in her accent, but in her friendly, outgoing nature, which shone through immediately.

'It's been a good few years since I called upon the services of someone like you,' I told her, while Ethan went to fetch Chase, 'so you'll have to guide me through it. Do I take part in the session?'

Grace shook her head. 'Nope, it's just me and the little guy. So where is best for us to go?' she asked, looking around, as if assessing the big open-plan space.

About which I had already given some thought. 'We've got a small front room,' I told her. 'Our "snug". Ethan doesn't normally use it. We've designated it out of bounds to all the kids.' I couldn't help but roll my eyes. '*We* don't usually use it either, to be honest. We've not been here that long and we keep forgetting about it! Anyway, you'll have some privacy in there, and I can get on with my cleaning.'

'Cleaning?' she said, her eyebrows shooting up. 'The place already looks spotless!'

'I'm a clean freak,' I admitted. 'It's a bit of an addiction.'

'An addiction I definitely *don't* have,' she said, laughing. 'And there's a thought. I don't live too far away from here, as it happens. So if you'd like my door keys …'

I laughed too. We were going to get along famously. As would also be the case, I hoped, for Ethan. Once he was back down with Chase, I showed them both into the snug (a treat for Ethan in itself) and left them to get on with whatever they'd be doing while I made a start on the bifold windows.

I knew little about the dark arts of play therapy. Back in the days when I'd been the Behaviour Unit manager in our local comprehensive school, it had been part of a range of therapeutic activities we'd do with some of our younger pupils, having them act out scenes using dolls and voices, or having them use painting as a way of expressing themselves. There was always meaning to be found, in their choice of setting and subject or, in painting, their use of shape and colour. I always found it fascinating but it wasn't really my area, and once I began fostering I had always been happy to leave such things to the experts.

Not that I'd really had much contact with play therapy since. I couldn't even remember when I had last used the service for help with a youngster, though I did recall discussing the role during one of my very early training sessions. While there were all kinds of professionals that could be brought in on a case, the play therapist's role was to do exactly that – play with a child, and, in doing so, help *them* learn how to play, either because they struggled with interacting with their peers in that way and/or had suffered trauma – abuse, particularly sexual, being a common one – that they were so traumatised by that they were unable to express their feelings verbally. Ethan obviously met this criteria on both counts, so perhaps that was why, following my call, he'd been prioritised.

Either way, it didn't matter. She was here, she was helping, and I had a whole hour free as a consequence, which meant it was time to bring out the big cleaning guns, in the form of the swanky new gadget Mike had bought me. It had been part of my birthday present and, though others might mock, clear evidence of how well my husband knew me. It was a thing of joy to me – a little electronic glass hoover. You simply sprayed the glass with some of the special cleaning solution provided, and then hoovered up all the liquid with the electric rubber squeegee. Brilliant!

At least, I had assumed it would be brilliant. In fact, it wasn't. It was worse than useless. I spent almost the full bloody hour trying to rub away the lines it created, and all the while I could hear my mother's voice over my shoulder. 'Load of rubbish, lass. You need newspaper and vinegar!'

With only minutes left before the session was due to end, I eventually gave up, threw down the stupid squeegee and made a cup of coffee instead. I could still hear rumbles of chat and laughter coming from the snug as I sat and enjoyed it, but as I rinsed out my mug, I was aware of them returning and, even before I turned around, I had this instinct that something had happened to make the atmosphere change.

I plucked up a tea towel and began to dry my hands as I turned around, noticing that Ethan had something in his hands as well. It was a large framed photograph from the snug, one of many I had in there.

'Everything okay?' I asked, thinking perhaps it had got broken. 'Is the glass cracked?' I went to reach for it, but Ethan pulled it against his chest.

'No,' Grace said. 'It's fine. Nothing to worry about. It's just that Ethan's a little confused.' She prised the photo away from Ethan slightly, enough so I could see it too. Though no way was he letting go of it, that much was obvious. Though he turned it enough that I could see it, he still held it firmly in two hands, proprietorially almost. Which seemed odd to me till Grace went on to explain. 'Here,' she said, pointing. 'That young man, there, on the right, see? The tall one. Ethan thinks it's his daddy.'

'It *is*,' Ethan said firmly. 'I told you. It *is* my daddy.'

Now he finally relinquished the picture, so I could take a proper look at it. It was one of many, many pictures I'd amassed over the years, both of my own kids and grandkids and our many foster children. This one, however, was a hybrid. It was a big group family photo, taken several years ago, at one of those big Christmas markets that had by then become all the rage. I remembered the day well. The whole market had been heaving and we'd taken refuge in the big, noisy, overheated *bierkeller*; several of us were holding mulled wine in little souvenir mugs, and the grandkids were holding over-sized pretzels. And it was all family, apart from the young man Ethan had pointed at. He was a former foster child. I did some quick mental maths. How old must he have been by then? Seventeen or eighteen?

'Why have *you*,' Ethan wanted to know, 'got a picture of my daddy?'

And then I saw it. And then I looked again at Ethan, and I *really* saw it. And then – whoosh! – came a torrent of memories and thoughts. And, as I began to take it in, the implications.

It can't be, was my first instinct, yet, realistically, *why* couldn't it? And the resemblance between the two now seemed so obvious. Not to just anybody, maybe, not on cursory inspection. But surely to *me*, who'd known that child since he'd been eleven.

'Do you know him?' Ethan asked. Grace was also looking at me quizzically.

'Ethan, sweetie,' I asked again, just to be sure. 'This is definitely your daddy?'

'I *told* you,' he said. 'It *is* him. It *is*!'

'So you *do* know him?' Grace asked. 'Ethan's dad? And didn't realise?' She gasped then, having clearly had a mind-boggling thought. 'Goodness,' she said. 'Is he a *relative* of yours?'

'Not exactly,' I said.

I stared at the smiling face again, and also at the past. Because if Ethan was right, it wasn't Jack he was looking at. It was Justin, the first child we'd ever fostered.

Could it really be that Ethan was his son?

Chapter 18

I must have gone into some kind of reverie because the next thing I was aware of was Grace gently touching my arm. 'So *is* it?' she was saying to me. 'Is this young man Ethan's daddy?'

Ethan was tugging at the picture again, keen to reclaim possession. 'It *is*,' he insisted again, as I handed it back to him.

'And I'm guessing you had no idea,' Grace added. 'Wow!'

Wow indeed. 'No,' I said, gathering my wits and my thoughts, and deciding there was no point in mentioning the name Justin at this point. Though the question remained – why had he changed it? 'But I suppose, when you think about it, it's not as unlikely as it might seem. We've been looking after children a long time. We've looked after a lot of children.' *And the likelihood that the children of children in care end up in care as well …*

It was one of those old chestnuts, which lots of people intuitively imagine is true. Children who've been in care have often had terrible starts in life, and, sadly, some scars never heal. So, in some cases, as adults, they also make poor choices, and the cycle of events that lead to ending up in care can so easily happen with *their* kids. I didn't even know if it was true, in fact. Or just a belief, widely held. Either way, it was a depressing thought, so I pushed it away. That line of thinking wasn't going to help anyone. 'Still, who'd have thought it, eh?' I said brightly, ruffling Ethan's hair and pointing towards the photo. 'And to think all this time that's been sitting in our snug!'

Grace glanced at her watch. 'Well, I'd better get on and leave you guys to chat. I'll write up the visit and send you a copy, but we had a good time, didn't we, Ethan? I'm thinking I'll come again Saturday – if that works for you, of course? – then stick with the Saturdays going forwards. Might as well be optimistic about school as not, don't you think?'

I agreed that it did work, appreciating that she was leaving us to it, as my mind was already teeming with questions, not least the approach I should now take with Ethan, and the fact that I needed to speak to Christine urgently, as this connection would need to be known. I couldn't think of any reason why it *needed* to change anything, but in my line of work, the god Protocol ruled, and could be capricious in myriad ways.

We saw Grace out, Ethan still keeping ownership of

the photograph, and I mused over the strength of the bond he and his father clearly shared, which had been forged over what? A sum total of around twenty to thirty visits, conducted so formally, and under scrutiny, in a prison?

Because that was the reality. Far from seeming gloomy, though, it actually lifted my spirits. Was blood thicker than water? My fostering experiences had often taught me 'no'. But there was no denying the bond Ethan and Jack/Justin shared. And even if a cynic might say both were being idealistic (the idea of a father, the idea of a son, rather than either actually living those roles), it seemed to me that, with a fair wind, and a lot of support, such ideas *could* become reality.

I smiled at Ethan. And there was now no denying of that reality. He was, in fact, so incredibly reminiscent of the photos I'd seen of Justin's younger brothers many years ago.

Though we didn't take Justin in till he was eleven years old, he'd been in the care of social services since he was five and a half, not much older than Ethan, when, having calmly removed his excrement-covered and starving younger siblings to safety, he had found a lighter and burned down the family home. (His mother was tracked down some streets away three hours later, having spent the day doing drugs with a 'friend'.) Since that day Justin had been shunted from pillar to post, with multiple failed placements, periods back with his mum and brothers – and then again rejected – before ending up with us, his last chance, before the misery of a secure children's home beckoned.

I pushed that second slew of unwelcome thoughts from my mind. The past could not be changed but the future was up for grabs, so, saddened as I was to know Justin had ended up in prison, I could mourn all that later. Right now, Justin's son was looking up at me impatiently, wanting answers. 'I tell you what,' I said. 'How about you and I go and sit down on the sofa and I'll tell you all about that photograph?'

Ethan followed me to the sofa and allowed me to snuggle up with him. He still had the photograph sitting in his lap.

'Your daddy, there' – I pointed – 'was about seventeen years old when this picture was taken, but that was long after he first came to stay with us. He was eleven then, still a little boy.'

'That's a *big* boy,' Ethan corrected.

'Well, yes, I suppose so, but to *us*, still a little boy, really – compared to this photograph anyway. And he came to live with us for a bit, just like you're doing now, till it was time for him to go and live somewhere else.'

'Did his mummy die too?' Ethan asked.

I caught my breath. 'No,' I said carefully. 'Your daddy's mummy didn't die. But she couldn't look after him, so that's why we did.'

I paused here, willing Ethan not to ask any more. I didn't want to lie to him, and I was also aware that

I Want My Daddy

I knew nothing of how much he knew about his father's childhood. And if it was as little as I suspected, it wouldn't be appropriate for me to be telling him more.

But he was clearly still thinking so I grabbed the advantage. 'We've had lots of little boys and girls live with us before you,' I went on. 'Some for a little while and some for a bit longer. It was a long time ago now that your daddy stayed with us, but even when he left us and became a grown-up himself, he was still like a part of our family. We used to see him at home, and sometimes go out for dinner, or on trips, like the one in the picture.' I squeezed his arm. 'Your daddy was very, very dear to us.'

Ethan was silent, staring at the photograph – it was obviously a lot to take in. Then he twisted his head up to look at me. 'So can he come and live with us, then? When he leaves the big house?'

I'm rarely stuck for words, especially when it comes to conversations with children, but this one – not least the sheer heart-tugging logic of it – really floored me. And not just because, to Ethan, it must have made such perfect sense. There was also the small matter that *nothing* yet was certain. We'd not even had the contact meeting with his grandparents yet, let alone any discussions about when or if he might go to live with them, or what role his dad was going to play in his life. And the last, the *very* last thing I wanted to do now was put anything into his head that might not happen. So I took my time and chose my words very carefully.

'I'm not sure what's going to happen when Daddy leaves the big house,' I told him. 'That's up to him, and he might have already made plans. Or have a new job he's going to work at that isn't close to where we live. But in the meantime, won't it be lovely when you next go to visit him and you can tell him you're living with me and Mike, just like he did when he was a little boy?'

'Big boy,' he corrected. Then he grinned. 'Was Daddy a good boy? He told me if I cheeked you and Mike, he'd give me what for. Not really,' he hurried on. 'Not bop me or anything. But he'd be very, *very* cross with me.' He put his small warm hand over mine. 'But I am a good boy, aren't I?'

'A *very* good boy,' I agreed. 'Now, would you like to keep that photograph? Put it up in your bedroom?'

'Yes,' he said, all enthused now. 'Shall we go and do it now? Then I can say nighty night to him at bedtimes.'

Which made my heart swell, but at the same time, I was relieved that we could end the line of questioning. At least till I'd been able to speak to someone and knew the new lie of the land.

I also had a million other questions. Just my luck, however, that Christine was on a day off when I tried to contact her, and Ethan's social worker, Lydia, was in court for the whole day. So without anyone to chew it over with, it was Mike who became my sounding board, the very moment Ethan went to bed that night.

'So, Jack being Justin is all making sense now. I mean, Jack was a groundsman, and Justin was a gardener, and both surnames are Davies, and, once you look at Ethan properly, they look so much alike. God, I'm amazed we didn't work it out before.'

'Why amazed? The idea never once crossed my mind. And to be honest, now it has, it's pretty mortifying. I mean, *jeez*, how can we have got so old, Case? And how can it be that we've been doing the job so long that we're now onto the second generation? Now actually fostering *the kids of the kids*? Good Lord, I mean, don't you feel ancient?'

'Not until you just pointed it out. So, big thanks for that, love. Remind me to put a face lift on my Christmas list.'

We both burst out laughing then. It was one of those times that you start out giggling, then you think about how funny it is and laugh a little harder, then before you know it, you're laughing hysterically because, well, because sometimes the most bizarre situations call for either hysterical laughter or a complete breakdown. We always tend to take the laughter.

The next day, though, it was back to business as usual and, though I still had Ethan at home with me, and obviously needed to keep him out of earshot, a post-breakfast *Paw Patrol* episode and a warm autumn morning meant I could speak to Christine in the garden, the other side of the bifold doors.

'I mean, Christ on a bike!' she declared after I'd told her everything. 'How mad is that? And, you know, I even remember the name on your files when I did the handover for you guys with John Fulshaw. I don't recall anyone ever having this happen before – do you?'

'No, never,' I said, 'but now I've thought about it, I reckon it probably happens more than people even realise. I mean, so many of the kids I've fostered have come from dysfunctional families, and what's the betting some of those parents were in care themselves as children? Plus, it's a small world, and most of the kids we look after come from our own authority, don't they? Perhaps now I'm properly ancient, as Mike told me last night, it's going to start happening all the time. But what now? How does this affect things? *Is* it going to alter anything?'

'I can't think why it would,' Christine said. 'Not in an adverse way, anyway. But how about you? It must have come as quite a shock.'

'Yes, and no. Yes at first because, well, who would have thought it? And it's funny, really, because if it hadn't been for Grace coming, we might never have known. We barely use that room ourselves, to be honest, and we decided to keep it that way for any foster kids – there's more than enough downstairs space anyway. But no, because once I thought about it, it all fitted immediately. We were in constant touch with Justin for several years after he left us, and when we lost touch it was because he became a gardener and moved away.'

'So you didn't keep in touch?'

'Oh, we would have, for sure. We still keep in touch with quite a few of our kids on social media. But if a kid loses touch with us, we tend not to chase. You know how it is, Chris; sometimes they need to leave their pasts behind and sometimes that includes us, because we are part of that past, aren't we? Though I'm not sure that was true of Justin – he just disappeared off the radar. And when kids do that we tend to think positive – that it's because they're getting on with their adult lives and don't need us anymore.' I sighed then. Christine obviously heard it.

'So this is pretty sad news for you, then,' she said.

It wasn't a question. 'Not as sad as it might have been,' I countered. 'He's coming out of prison, he's got a son he loves, he has a reason to sort his life out. The best reason in the world to sort his life out, in fact. God, I *really* hope it works out. I mean, I did anyway, for Ethan's sake, but now I know who his dad is, it matters even more. Honestly, Chris, if you knew the half of it … What that lad went through when he was Ethan's age … I won't bore you with it now. I know you're busy. But let's just say, if you were the kind of person who already didn't have much faith in human nature …'

'I hear you, Casey. But, between us, we'll do our absolute utmost to help make that happen, won't we? I have no idea how hard that's likely to be with the grand-parents – that's Lydia's department – but if they have any sense they will surely see that, if Jack *does* come good, it can only be beneficial for Ethan to have him in his life, can't it? Actually, given the bond Ethan clearly has with his father, I'd argue that it would be positively detrimental if they try to stop them continuing to see one another.'

'And I have to believe Jack/Justin can come good for Ethan. I *do* believe he can. I know it's been years since I've seen him but you only need to look at the case notes to see how committed he is to the boy. He's been there for him – and yes, I know he could hardly go anywhere, but there's nothing to set alarm bells ringing, is there? And the reason he is in prison, remember, is because he found out he had a son, and, more than that, saw the conditions in which he was living. Which is not to say ...' Realising I was waffling on now, I regrouped. 'God, wait, sorry, Chris, listen to me rattling on! The main point is, can I see Justin? Will I be allowed to visit him? And does he even realise it's us fostering Ethan?'

'I don't know the answer to your second question, and to the first, I don't see why not, but hold on. Let me talk to managers before you make any moves, just so I can cover your backside if we're about to breach any protocols. I'm not sure you would be – it's not like you're planning to get in touch with an unknown parent, and Justin slash Jack has obviously played a huge part in your life. But just let me check first, okay?'

'Okay,' I said, feeling impatient already. When I get something in my head, I like to act upon it immediately, not wait around for permission from the Protocol over-lords. But it was what it was, and, like I'd said, it wasn't as if Justin – no, *Jack* now – was going anywhere. But I was itching to find out if he knew Ethan was with us, and also why he'd changed his name. Had Jack emerged because Justin had got into serious trouble and was on the run? I hoped not but till I saw him, I wouldn't know.

'I understand,' I told Christine, 'But the sooner the better. Now I know, I want to know more. I need to know more. And I need to see him. I know it sounds a bit arrogant – though it's not meant to be – but I believe Mike and I can really make a difference here. If Justin – *Jack* – has us in his corner it will really bolster him. I just *know* it.'

'Leave it with me,' Christine said. 'I promise I'll be fast, and in the meantime try to put it out of your mind. Ethan has the visit with the grandparents tomorrow, right?'

Right indeed. Though amid the events of the last twenty-four hours I had almost forgotten all about it. 'Oh yes, yes he has. I'm taking him down at two … And there's a thought: Ethan might say something to them about his dad, mightn't he?'

'Ah, I hadn't thought of that. Yes, I suppose he might. Let me have a word with Lydia about that, what they're up to speed about, and how we might play things going forward. Forewarned is forearmed so perhaps they need to be made aware in advance. It shouldn't make any difference to anything in theory, but it *is* somewhat sensitive, given they're ambivalent towards him. We wouldn't want them thinking we're in cahoots with him or anything, or aim to pressure them re future regular contact with Jack. You know how funny people can be about things like that. I mean, I know that's precisely the scenario we *are* hoping will happen, but they need to feel they have some agency and aren't just being directed by us. It's important *they* build that relationship with him, and at their pace. No, you just carry on as you are. I'll catch Lydia this evening and run all this by her. I think she *will* probably think it prudent to fill them in before you and Ethan get there, especially if you're going to have a few minutes with them at the end. Either way, I'll text you, okay?'

I might tell my waking self to put everything to one side and just carry on as I am, as Christine had directed, but there was nothing I could do about my sleeping self. That night, as I half-expected, my dreams were filled with Justin. I kept waking up through the night remembering little snippets of the times we had shared with him, and it took all my self-control not to wake Mike and run them all by him, especially when one particular memory hit me like a steam train.

Spaghetti-bollock-naked. Of *course*! When Ethan had said it a few days ago, yes, I'd known I'd heard the term before, but had automatically attributed it to Tyler. He was the master of the silly expression, after all. But something else surfaced; the fact that he'd heard it from somewhere else. It might have been Kieron – it was a long time ago now – but, equally it might have been Justin himself. Because the image, so long buried, was now pin-sharp in my head. I could see Justin now, wooden spoon in his hand, a blue and white striped chef's apron round his waist. It was way too big for him – I remembered that bit particularly – reaching to the floor, and puddling round his stockinged feet. He was helping me cook dinner, and pretending to be one of the then famous TV chefs, an expressive Italian man called Gino D'Acampo.

'I am a-cooking,' he trilled, 'My a-Italian a-spezziality! It eez a-spaghetti bollock naked!'

We'd laughed. We'd laughed hard. We'd almost laughed until we cried. And not just because it was funny, or because it was such a sweet, unexpected moment, but also because of just how much it had meant to us. It was a moment of unscripted, unremarkable everyday family fun, of a kind Justin, who had been born into such wretchedness, had never known before.

And it had mattered to him too. Because he had passed it on to Ethan. It was a lovely thought with which to drift back off to sleep.

Chapter 19

I was up at the crack of dawn along with Mike on Friday morning, determined to start the day as I meant to go on: in an optimistic, coffee-fuelled way. Today was so important, it just *had* to go well.

'Ah,' Mike said, the penny dropping about my uncharacteristic pre-dawn start. (At this time of year, I almost never beat the birds.) 'It's the visit with Nannie Whatshername and Grandpa Grumps today, then, is it?'

'Bloody idiot!' I joked. 'It's Grannie Jo and Pops. Or so I'm told. AKA Jocelyn and Alan Baines. And yes, we're setting off around half one, to be there in plenty of time for the 2.00 p.m. meeting. I'm guessing someone might want to have a quick word with me before they go in, given what's happened in the last twenty-four hours.'

I'd been lucky only having to travel ten minutes to this particular contact centre because, more often than not, when it came to contact visits, I'd have to drive miles out of town. And that wasn't just social services making things difficult. Most of the time it was because the circumstances were such that it was important that the birth family didn't know the location where their child or children were placed. And, in the minority of cases where such things weren't a consideration, I still usually ended up driving a fair way because it was difficult for the parents, financially or otherwise, to travel any distance to see their children.

This wasn't the case for Mr and Mrs Baines. Indeed, they'd made clear that, despite Mr Baines's impediment, they'd be the ones who would make the journey to the contact centre so that I, and their little grandson, didn't have to; a positive sign that they were already looking out for him. Another was that they seemed to be adapting well to Mr Baines's new disability. Mrs Baines drove, and Christine told me that they were already pretty adept at getting her husband's wheelchair in and out of the boot. Which might not seem a big deal – they were hardly elderly, after all – but taking on a five-year-old was no small thing to do, so any signs of resilience and robustness, such as this, were obviously music to my ears.

Fond of routine as I was, I let Ethan sleep in. He had a big day ahead of him after all. And, by the time he came down, at around half past eight, was already finishing up my cereal. 'Hungry?' I asked, gesturing for him to come and join me at the breakfast bar. 'You want my raisin and honey wheats, sweetie, or the chocolate hoops today?'

To which he floored me by replying, in an 'I've already-thought-this-through' tone, 'I don't want to see my grannie and pops today, Casey. They shouted at my mummy. I just want my daddy.'

I took a moment to digest just how firm had been this statement. He was so young still. He had been so much younger when he'd last seen them. How could he *possibly* have any such memories? Or, more likely to my mind, was this something he'd been told?

'Oh, sweetheart,' I said. 'I know you want your daddy, and, you know, I think you'll be able to see him more often soon. And it won't be that long before he moves out of that place and then you'll be able to see him lots and lots. But Grannie and Pops love you, darling, and I know it's been a long time, but when you were a little boy, you loved them too. You just don't really remember.'

I knew I was making this up as I went along, but from all I'd heard from Christine, not least from Mrs Baines herself, the grandparents and Ethan *had* had a relationship, so that bond must have been there at some stage. And now it was my job to push Ethan towards it. As things stood, it was his best chance of a brighter future.

Having coaxed a decision out of him – the raisin wheats, unexpectedly – I poured out a bowl, added milk, and then set it before him, while he scrambled up onto the adjacent bar stool.

'Dig in,' I said, 'and while you're eating, I'll explain what's going to happen this afternoon, okay? What you can expect.'

He looked up at me anxiously. 'Aren't you going to be there?'

'I am absolutely going to be there,' I reassured him. 'Though I'm not sure if I'm allowed in while you meet Grannie and Pops, I'll be close by, so don't worry. And I do know that Heather who takes you to see Daddy will be there too, so you won't be on your own with them. Oh, and Lydia might be there as well. You remember Lydia? The nice lady who came to see you when you first came to stay with us? She's your social worker.'

'So Heather will stay with me?'

'Absolutely,' I said again, and this seemed to relax him a little. So while he spooned some cereal into his mouth, I pushed on. 'I bet Grannie Jo and Pops are so excited to see you. I bet they won't believe what a big boy you are now!'

He stopped chewing and swallowed. 'Will they think I'm still a three or do you think they'll know I'm a five now?'

I was puzzled for a moment but quickly realised he was talking about his age; perhaps he had been three the last time they'd seen each other.

'Well, as you're so big now, I think they might even think that you're a *six*! I mean, look at those muscles of yours. You're such a big boy.'

I Want My Daddy

Ethan dropped his spoon into his bowl and carefully rolled up both pyjama sleeves. He then flexed like a bodybuilder. 'I'll tell them I'm going to be a six at my birthday, shall I? They might buy me some presents.'

'They might indeed,' I agreed, laughing. How quickly kids, with all their pragmatism, could get to the bottom line. Potential crisis over, we finished our breakfast chatting about who might be the strongest person in the whole wide world. Which, of course, was his daddy because apparently his daddy could 'swing me up onto his shoulders, all in one go, and without ever dropping me, even once'. And now I knew what I knew, this held even more meaning. The Justin we'd first met had been a strong, strapping boy, and since his tendency, when in pain, was to lash out indiscriminately, he'd come to us with a depressing reputation. He was too much, too violent, too angry, too volatile, his emotional frailty getting more and more hard to connect with under all those layers of opprobrium. To think of him now, to visualise that strength redirected to playing with his son, was enough to bring a lump to my throat.

After dressing Ethan, and allowing him a little time on his iPad while I made us both some lunch, I began to feel nerves kicking in. Where Ethan seemed, by now, to be looking at the trip out as nothing more than that, I was becoming ever more aware of how much rested on this first encounter. Was I being naïve in setting such store by that blood connection? Didn't parents neglect and abandon their children all the time? What was to say that they wouldn't take one look at Ethan and decide, even if reluctantly, that he'd be a bit too much for them? Supposing he kicked off, for whatever reason, and their best intentions vaporised as a result? Just as a child who'd always nagged for a puppy might baulk when the hard work of walking it became evident, might Ethan's grandparents compare the idea with the reality and decide the latter might prove harder than they'd thought?

I was also anxious about what they had or hadn't been told. I hoped Christine had managed to run everything by them, but even if she had, might I still face a barrage of uncomfortable questions? I also prayed that the knowing wouldn't negatively impact on their decision to possibly foster Ethan long-term. Like Christine, I didn't really see why it should, but you could never second-guess how someone else might think.

By the time we set off, then, I had the same sort of jitters that I remembered having way back, going into school to sit my end-of-year exams.

The local family centre was one I hadn't been into in a long while and by the looks of it, nothing had changed. Like several I'd visited over the years, this one kept its secrets close. A big old sprawling Victorian house, presumably bought by the council many years previously, there was little on the outside to suggest the sort of services it provided. Which was intentional, obviously – no sense adding to the distress of parents and carers who, for whatever reason, were forced to have any contact with their children in this complicated way, under the close supervision of civil servants.

I pulled in, and drove down the long narrow drive that led to the property's back garden. Which was no longer a garden but a visitors' car park. Where the first thing I saw once I'd parked and clambered out was a man in a wheelchair. And, unless the laws of coincidence had recently been re-written, I presumed it was Alan Baines. It surely had to be. He was missing a foot.

He was vaping, spewing huge clouds of custard-scented vapour that I could smell even at a distance, and, for a moment, unsure whether to approach him (he might have snuck out, and not want Ethan to see him vaping), I considered trotting right past and leaving him to it – we'd be meeting soon enough, after all. But he didn't look coy about it – in fact, he didn't seem to even notice. He was too busy looking hard at Ethan.

'My God,' he said, as we drew closer. 'The apple doesn't fall far from the tree, does it? Hello, lad,' he said to Ethan, who squeezed my hand extra tightly. 'I'm your pops, and I'd recognise you anywhere.'

'Mr Baines!' I said brightly, through the sweet veil between us. 'You recognise right, doesn't he, Ethan? And I'm Casey. Very nice to meet you at last.'

Ethan surprised me then by offering his own 'Hello', closely followed by, 'What you done with your foot? Did you fall off your bike? I did that when I was little, but they never chopped it off.'

215

Cringing ever so slightly at the bluntness of Ethan's words, I watched as his grandfather absorbed this. Initially looking stunned, he recovered very quickly, his face cracking into a grin that turned into a laugh. 'Not my bike, lad. I was being chased by lions in the forest, and though I managed to beat most of them off once I'd climbed up a tree, the biggest one – the boss lion – got me. Clean took my foot off, and in one single bite!'

Ethan's face was a picture of awe and respect. '*Awesome*,' he said. 'Can I tell that to Miss Peachie?'

'One of Ethan's teachers,' I told Mr Baines, laughing too. 'And I suppose we best be getting inside,' I added. 'Do you need some help getting back in, or …?'

'Just hold the doors open, lovey, I'll be fine,' Mr Baines said, still smiling and winking at Ethan. He was a large man with thick hair, now mostly gone grey and though I didn't know his exact age – early sixties was my best guess – what I could see was that he had once been a strong, confident man, just by the way he carried himself. I could also see his pride, and the effort he'd put in, as he expertly manoeuvred his wheelchair around and back inside through the double doors.

'*There* you are,' said a woman who was approaching down the corridor. 'I was beginning to think you'd taken root out there! The social worker's here, and –' She stopped abruptly then, having clapped eyes on Ethan. 'Oh,' she said, 'oh!' then she sunk down to her knees. 'Oh, look at the size of you!' She spread her arms wide. 'Oh, come here, my baby boy!'

I Want My Daddy

She was close enough to attempt to throw her arms around Ethan but, perhaps understandably, he stepped back in shock, leaving her with nothing to hold on to, and her eyes now moist with tears.

Happily, however, she soon recovered her composure. 'Look at me,' she said, shaking her head and standing up again. 'Take no notice. I'm just being a right silly sausage. I'm your Grannie Jo, Ethan, love. D'you remember me?'

Ethan's grip on my hand didn't lessen one iota. 'Are you going to say hi,' I urged brightly, 'like you did with your pops?'

I could see Grannie Jo was still quite overcome. And why, I reasoned, wouldn't she be emotionally fragile? She'd not long lost her daughter so she'd almost always be on the edge anyway, and now, faced with the grandson from whom she'd been estranged for so long, what else would she be *but* emotional? It hit me that that this wasn't just about them accepting Ethan. It was every bit as much about him accepting *them*. Even if that wasn't exactly how the law saw it, they needed to earn his love too.

Ethan, perhaps shocked, had still yet to answer my question, so the arrival of Lydia Heptonstall was a welcome diversion. 'Ah!' she said cheerily, '*there* you all are! Are we all ready? The room's just come free, so we're set to go in. And, Casey, do you know where the waiting area is? Though we're talking two hours so if you'd prefer to go shopping ...'

Ethan's hand gripped mine tighter. 'You're going to stay, you said,' he whispered.

'I did and I am, sweetie. I'll be right here for when you're done.'

'What about Heather? Where's Heather? If you're not allowed, I want Heather to come with me.'

I looked at Lydia with raised eyebrows. 'She's imminent,' she said. 'Just been held up in the office but she'll be here any minute.' She held her hand out to Ethan in a no-nonsense manner, and, with my gentle urging, he transferred his trust, his sense of security, from my hand to hers.

I leaned down and gave him a quick peck on the forehead. 'I won't go anywhere,' I said. 'I'll be right here, I promise. But you'll have fun –' I glanced up and smiled at the Baineses. 'I know you will. You'll be absolutely fine.'

I watched them all head off then, feeling glad that the ice had been broken, that Ethan had met them with the security of having me by his side. I could only hope they could now build on that first positive encounter, aided – ably, I trusted – by Lydia and, once she arrived and joined them, Heather. Even so, it felt odd, and would always feel odd, that the person he naturally felt closest to right now was not to be part of the visit.

Thankfully, the waiting area had a bookcase filled with various second-hand books, because, after shopping – off the agenda, obviously – reading is my second favourite hobby. So I got myself as comfortable as I could on the faux leather (i.e. sweaty-looking

PVC-covered) sofa, and settled down to read what I could of the murder mystery I'd selected, having first established with the receptionist that I'd be allowed to take it home – no way was I going to get immersed if I was going to have to leave it behind.

Thankfully, it was one of those 'pick it up and you can't put it down kinds of books' so, barring a brief distraction when Heather arrived, ten minutes in, I was, for the most part, far, far away, on a windswept beach, somewhere up in the Scottish Highlands. So involved was I by then with the machinations of the irritable police detective that, when the two hours were up and Lydia came in to get me, it felt like no more than half an hour had passed.

To my delight, she was grinning from ear to ear. 'Would you like to come in and join us all while Ethan says goodbye?' she asked. 'A bit of a rocky start – he was really, really shy with them – but once Heather arrived, he got his mojo back immediately, and a good time, as they say, has been had by all. In fact, I think he's completely exhausted them.' She saw my anxious expression then and grinned. 'In a *good* way,' she added. 'Not an "OMG, do we think we can really *do* this?" kind of way. In fact, I'd go so far as to say that, to my mind, at any rate, it's gone even better than expected.'

'That is *so* good to hear,' I said, popping the paperback in my handbag. 'So what now? Is the next visit likely to be soon? Be good to build on this success pronto, wouldn't it?'

And there was no question that the visit had been a success. Mrs Baines was still tearful, but a good kind of tearful, and Ethan's earlier reticence around his grand-parents now seemed to be forgotten, as he hugged both of them hard as they gave him a final kiss.

'Can you help push Pops outside?' Grannie Jo said to him eventually, 'while I have a quick word with Casey?'

I looked towards Lydia, who nodded her approval, and then waited till Ethan was out of sight.

Jocelyn Baines didn't beat around the bush. 'I know all about your history with Jack now,' she said, 'so I know you'll feel differently about him than we do. But I couldn't leave without being straight with you, because I'm sure you can appreciate our own history with him was very different. And not so good. I know Ethan has an ongoing relationship with him, and I respect that, and I also know he's due out of prison soon. I'm just saying that, no matter what, he has quite a way to go with us before we can start thinking about building bridges. We have to think of Ethan and what's likely to be best for him in the future. The kind of people he has, or should have, in his life. And whether –' She paused, but her chin jutted slightly. 'Well, given how young he is, some relationships he'd be better off without, if he's to have a future with us. That's all I wanted to say. Just so you know where we stand. I really hope you understand.'

Which was quite the speech. Straight to the point, calmly delivered and clearly very heartfelt. Mrs Baines, and Mr Baines too, presumably, had obviously been thinking about this a *lot*. I composed myself the best I could, so I could answer her equally frankly.

'Of course I understand,' I said, 'and thank you for being straight with me. I wouldn't have expected anything else. This has all come as quite a shock to us too, as you can imagine. We know Jack as Justin, of course, and we took care of him for a good while. And we love him ...' I added, noting the slight widening of her eyes. 'So to find out where he's at ... what he's done ... and to learn he's Ethan's father ...' I spread my hands. 'But it doesn't change anything as far as all this is concerned. I know he's had his problems, and his issues, and I'm not going to try and make a case for him to you. In fact, I completely agree with you that you have to think of Ethan's best interests – so do we all – which means you have to weigh all these things up. There's obviously a great deal to work out between you all. I just hope it *can* be worked out. For Ethan's sake.'

Mrs Baines nodded. 'As do we. Our daughter was our world, and it almost killed us that she died before we had the chance to make things right. That in itself is a huge load to carry, believe me, so I'm not going to throw stones from glass houses. And I know it wasn't Jack's fault directly, what happened to our Brogan, but everything started when they got together. *Everything bad.* If she had never laid eyes on him ...'

She stopped then, and I could see she'd been ambushed by a wave of grief and was struggling to contain her emotions so I definitely didn't want to get into a blame game, and could absolutely understand why she would see Justin as the catalyst for her daughter's downfall and death. And who was I to say if that were true or not, in any case? I reached out and placed my hand on her arm.

'I'm so sorry for your loss,' I said. 'I can't begin to imagine how you are coping with it all. But I'm happy, *so* happy, that you are getting to reconnect with Ethan, and I'm sure if we all work together on this, then everything will come together eventually, one way or another.'

Mrs Baines placed her hand over mine. 'I really hope so. Take care of our boy. He's all we have now. He's … well, you know. I don't need to spell it out, do I?'

I reassured her I did know, and that I would take good care of her grandson, and we went our separate ways; her to their car, flanked by Lydia and Heather, and me and Ethan to my car and home.

In contrast to his grandmother, and oblivious to the bigger picture, Ethan was positively buzzing. His pops had bought him a toy helicopter and he declared it was his best toy in the whole wide world. He chatted all the way home about the things they had said and done, and about how much he was looking forward to the next visit – not least the prospect of benefitting hugely from this whole new avenue of potential presents. It was almost as if he'd completely forgotten his stark assessment of his grandparents that very morning. But then, I reasoned, he was five, and in his five-year-old world, tomorrow, and its problems, were a world away. He lived in the present and for the present things were fine.

I tried my utmost to keep up with the conversation, nodding and oohing and aahing at appropriate points, but all I could think about was another boy, Justin, for whom the future was probably something very much at the forefront of his here and now, while he waited in the 'big house' for his release date. Ethan's grandparents weren't just going to smile and play happy families with him – Mrs Baines had been abundantly clear on that – even if the law said – as it did and does – that, all other things being equal, he held all the rights as the surviving parent. At least, in theory. If he took them on over custody, I had a hunch it would backfire. No, he was going to have to work for it, perhaps for his relationship with Ethan to even *exist*, even if he felt none of it was his fault.

Trouble was that the Justin I remembered wasn't likely to take this on the chin. For all that he'd done wrong, he had always had a strong sense of justice. If the Baines decided they wanted him out of Ethan's life – and I had to concede, given their loss, that they might well do exactly that – would he respond like with like? I knew there was a real risk of that happening if and when they became Ethan's carers and were therefore in control. Those words of Mrs Baines – *I have to think about the kind of people Ethan has, or should have, in his life, about relationships he might be better off not having* – were a potent reminder that this wouldn't be easy.

No, to get what was left of Ethan's family to actually become one was always going to be a hard ask, for anyone. Not without a great deal of support and guidance. And patience. This kind of Rome definitely wasn't built in a day. And could so easily come crashing down.

Chapter 20

On the Monday, following the first contact session with Ethan's grandparents, I was a woman on a mission. And the first item on my mission schedule was to call Mrs McKendrick and somehow persuade her that it was simply not good enough that Ethan was still not back in his classroom. His life was just about to become more structured in so many ways and I felt it was important that his education went hand in hand with that. He needed the routine, and I didn't mind admitting that I needed some precious hours where I wasn't constantly running around after a hyperactive five-year-old.

This wasn't just me being bolshy. Or even trying to put my fears about Justin's tenuous position out of my mind. As promised, Grace the play therapist had returned on the Saturday morning for the second of her play sessions with Ethan. And though she'd emerged from that and had to zoom straight off to another appointment, she'd called me later and pretty much spelled all that out to me. In her professional opinion, Ethan didn't really need a play therapist as much as he needed the routines and structure of a school day and, hand in hand with that, other children to play *with*. She went one step further: she felt there was nothing about Ethan, albeit in her limited experience, that would preclude him from being in a mainstream school, as long as he had sufficient support put in place.

She'd also, hence her wish to talk everything through with me, hit upon what she thought was probably the reason Ethan was so scared of blood. It was all down to computer games, she told me. She even rattled off the list of three or four of such games, a couple of which I'd never heard of but one I definitely had; one so notorious for its violence and brutality and gore that I was at a loss to know why even *adults* would want to play it.

'He said he'd often be "babysat" by a neighbour's son in the evenings – this being at their house, and not his own. His mum would be downstairs with them, presumably drinking or using recreational drugs, and he'd be put to bed in this teenager's room, but of course he wasn't in bed and he definitely wasn't sleeping. He'd basically watch this lad play for hours on end, and on one of those enormous monitors – he described it to me as being half the wall. He said he'd drift off, wake up and hear the sounds of people screaming, and see blood spattered everywhere, and people exploding and having arms and legs blown off, and then, of course, he'd have horrible nightmares. He said he often woke up and couldn't work out where he was, and that sometimes he'd think he was dreaming and wasn't. And what runs through it all is that Mum wasn't there, and he often went to sleep really, really scared.'

So, in addition to being put in his own bed, with only his iPad and its precious timer, now this to contend with as well. No wonder the poor mite was terrified. Glad as I was to get to the bottom of it, I was sickened. And it was difficult to square my compassion for his young mother with my astonishment that, even if drugs *did* play a part in her behaviour, this girl had thought that this was okay. It just went to show how normalising drug use really did distort everything.

But there was nothing to be done except consign it to the past and hope that Ethan's terrors would begin to lessen as he grew older and was no longer exposed to such things. The important thing now, and Grace's revelations made my conviction even stronger, was that this five-year-old start living the *life* of a five-year-old. And Grace's comments and advice were, without question, useful weapons. The school urgently needed to put things in place so that they *could* look after Ethan adequately; they had a budget to do this and it seemed unfair to me that they had seemed reluctant to do this early on. And now I had my ammo and was all locked and loaded, I was ready for a verbal fight, if need be.

I was knocked for six, then, when, as soon as I was put through to Mrs McKendrick, it was she who put that very point to *me*.

'You've beaten me to it,' she said chattily. 'I was going to call you in a bit myself. We actually met to discuss Ethan on Friday afternoon, and we're agreed it'll be fine for him to return. You can bring him in this morning if you like to. Or tomorrow, of course, if that's too short notice.'

'Oh, right,' I said, completely unprepared for this U-turn. 'What's changed? I mean, don't get me wrong, I am one hundred per cent grateful. But why the turnabout? Did something change?'

'Indeed it did. We've managed to free up a full-time teaching assistant, Miss Peachie. I think she's worked with Ethan already, hasn't she, in the short time he's been with us? Anyway, she normally helps out in Years 3 and 4 for half the week, but we have managed to get a new TA, just started this morning.' She chuckled then. 'I don't need to tell you, Casey, do I, that they are like gold dust right now? Anyway, he's going to be working with the older children, which means that Ethan and one other child will have Miss Peachie to themselves for the full week.'

'So, not one-to-one then?' I asked, feeling slightly crestfallen at this news. 'Will Ethan always be with this other child too?'

'No, no, it's not going to work like that, don't worry. The other child's in the same year, but in a different group, so we've divided up the timetable so that both get the one-to-one attention they need, *when* they need it. And given Ethan's triggers seem to happen mostly during breaks, and at lunchtime, and during the lessons directly after, that's when we've scheduled the one-to-ones for him. But it's early days, and once it's in place we can tweak, if we need to, as we go. The main thing is that we have a plan, as I'm sure you'll agree.'

I very much did agree, and said so. This was brilliant news indeed. And best of all, I didn't have to go in all guns blazing, potentially creating discord. What I would have liked to ask, and didn't, because I knew Mrs McKendrick was busy, was what had really brought about this sudden change in direction. Surely it wasn't just because a new TA had started. Had they been working hard behind the scenes to try and accommodate Ethan? Or had some pressure been applied by Lydia or Christine?

I'd have liked to have known, but either way, it didn't matter. Ethan was going back to school, to normality, and that was what mattered, though rather than dash around chivvying him straight there right now, which might distress him, I told Mrs McKendrick I'd bring him back in the following morning. That would at least give me a chance to prepare him for re-entry.

I needn't have worried. When I told him he'd be going back to school tomorrow, it was as if the traumas of the past had never happened.

'Yes!' he whooped, with an exuberant fist pump. 'I get to play with my bestest friends again tomorrow. I'm gonna take my helicopter and show it to CJ and Charlie, if it's okay? Is it? Will they let me?'

I grinned. 'Well, you aren't officially supposed to bring toys into school. But since this is such a special toy, from your pops, I think we might just sneak it into your bag, and I'll ask Miss Peachie if it's okay to show it to CJ and Charlie at playtime.'

So, a result. And an unexpectedly easy one. Next on my agenda was a phone call to Lydia Heptonstall, to see what further feedback there might have been following that first contact visit, and whether anything had changed re the Baineses' original intention to start off by fostering Ethan long-term. From my own feedback, notwithstanding Mrs Baines's chilling comments regarding Justin, I couldn't imagine that they would have changed their minds. It seemed so clear to me that they wanted to forge a future with their little grandson.

I was also keen to hear if there had been any objections to the idea of Mike and I going to visit Justin personally. So as soon as Ethan was settled on the sofa with a snack and an episode of *Paw Patrol*, I was on the phone, quick as you like.

'Your optimism has not turned out to be misplaced,' Lydia told me. 'In fact, I had a lovely email from Mrs Baines on Friday evening, saying how overjoyed they both are to have Ethan back in their lives and how much they wanted to make a new life for him with them.'

'That's great,' I said, if thinking privately '... and his father?' but I figured it best to park that one for now. 'So they're still keen to forge ahead with the fostering assessment?'

'Oh, more than that,' Lydia said. 'In fact, Jo confirmed over the weekend that they didn't want to go through the official channels. They want to take Ethan as his grandparents and rightful guardians.'

I felt a twitch of anxiety tremble my antennae. 'What? Can they do that?'

'Technically, and if they really pushed, of course they could,' Lydia explained. 'However, I pointed out that we'd already started the process, and that it wouldn't take much longer, but that it was really in their interest to let us go through the courts. They will need that backing and stability if – and I know you won't like this, Casey, given your personal connection to him – but if Jack came out of prison and were to suddenly decide that he wanted to take Ethan himself.'

'I don't think he'd do that,' I immediately said. But then thought to myself, *why wouldn't he*? I didn't have the first clue what he was thinking. All I knew was how often Ethan talked of going to live with Daddy when he left his 'big house'. How much of that was coming from Justin? Any? Or was it just pie-in-the-sky stuff to make his son feel secure with him? But would he really be so rash as to go down that road straight out of prison? He would surely realise he couldn't even give Ethan a home, yet alone provide financially for his needs. 'Surely he wouldn't do that? Surely he would see Ethan would be better off with his grandparents, at least in the short term, and possibly for his whole childhood? I mean, I don't know his circumstances, but when he first gets out of prison, he'll need to find somewhere to live, and get a job, and get set up, and ...'

'I.e. you probably *do* know his circumstances, or did, certainly his background, and can probably predict better than I can what he'll be up to. And for what it's worth, I imagine he's likely to see sense. But we don't *know* that, and the reason I'm advising the Baines the way I am is that if a judge has already made an order about where Ethan lives, then even his dad couldn't prevent that. And it won't really make a difference to them if we got that. They will still be his grandparents, but they will have social services in the background for quite some time, able to offer support. I know a lot of parents and grandparents don't like that level of scrutiny, but at the end of the day it's in Ethan's best interests, and they know that, at least for the next year or so. Belt and braces, that's the thinking. Pre-empt discord.'

'I agree,' I said, because, despite my private concerns around poor Justin and what might happen to his contact, this *was* in Ethan's best interests, no question. 'And I'm hoping that you won't see our ties with Justin – or Jack, sorry. I must remember that – as a conflict of interest? I'm guessing Christine has told you we intend to go visit him in prison, but honestly, to us, this is no different to building a relationship with any birth parent. We've always done it, and yes, the circumstances are different this time because we fostered the parent, but actually, we think this is even *more* of a reason to keep in touch, and help build the bridges needed in order for Ethan's future to be happy and full.'

Lydia burst out laughing. 'Did you write that up and memorise it?' she said. 'Christine said you were a hard sell, Casey,' she continued, still chuckling. 'But you don't need to worry. We're not taking you on here. It's no different from what we ask of foster carers all the time, so no, we don't have objections to your visiting him. And who knows, even given that you must remain neutral, you might be helpful with the diplomacy side of things.'

And we'd certainly need *lots* of diplomacy, I thought. However much of an uphill struggle it might be, every fibre of my being was committed to the principle that Ethan needed his dad in his life every bit as much as his grandparents.

But I was getting ahead of myself, gushing on then about how soon we could visit the prison and how we could maybe be the ones to take Ethan for his next visit and spare Heather a journey.

Lydia waited till I'd finished before saying, 'Whoa, hold your horses! We first have to request a visiting order for you. And then you have to wait until you receive it – I think they come through via email these days. And Jack then has to *agree* to your visit, and sign off both of your names, and *then* you'll get a date when you can go. It will obviously be on a Sunday, so it can coincide with Ethan's visit, but other than that, once you've got it through, you'll be good to go.'

I was a little deflated to hear all of that, and in my head I was thinking it might take weeks. But the very next day, not long after I'd dropped Ethan off at school, I received an unexpected text from Christine:

Dead simple process. VO applied for online, and approved within the hour. You're on the next visit, this Sunday. Let me know how it goes! C x

It was fair to say that I was over the moon to receive that, not least because it dispelled that little kernel of doubt that Justin – no, *Jack* – would actually want to see us. But I was still nervous. Him wanting to see us didn't necessarily mean he still had good feelings about us. It was him who'd lost touch, there was no doubt about that, but what if he'd expected us to try and find *him*? Nothing in the preceding years had hinted that might be true, but kids who've had hard starts can have funny fixations. It could well be that he didn't have the where-withal to ask us for help, but, given his background, it could be that the fact that we hadn't pushed things made him think we'd abandoned him, just like his mother had. You really couldn't ever second-guess these things.

'STOP IT!' Mike insisted after I'd run all these thoughts past him – the very minute after I'd put Ethan to bed that night, after a (so far so good, I wasn't count-ing my chickens) calm and debacle-free first day back at school. 'Case, love, you're talking utter rot! You know how we've always played it. The kids who leave us know they always have a family here, they know they only need to reach out, and even when we've moved house, it's never made a difference, has it? They always, *always* know how to find us, because you've got more WhatsApp groups than probably Justin bloody Bieber. And Facebook, and TikTok, and Messenger. There isn't a kid in the world that can't find you if they need you. We do the same with all of them. You *know* this. When the time comes, and they drift away, we assume they've made their own lives, and we don't – and we're right not to – pressure them. We stay in the background, unless they want us in their foreground. Honestly, Case, love, you *know* all this.'

Mike was right: I did know. It had always been that way. I just felt so guilty that I'd been bumbling along all this time, thinking Justin must be living a happy life, and all the time his actual life had become totally wretched. Having to run away from drug dealers. Relationship asunder. And then locked away in prison. And all of that time we'd been just a phone call away. He knew that. Why on earth hadn't he reached out to us?

Well, I guessed I was soon going to find out.

Chapter 21

It had been decided that to keep things normal for Ethan, he would travel to the prison in Heather's car, as usual, while Mike and I would go in Mike's car, separately. That way, we could follow the plan usually in place, and set off back home once we'd had our chat with Justin, leaving Ethan to finish his visit in peace with his dad. The plan – quite a loose plan given the distance involved – was that the four of us, once arrived, would assemble in the prison car park, then sign in and go in together. Mike and I would then head off to meet Justin first while Heather and Ethan stayed and played in the waiting area.

'There's a kids' play area,' Heather explained on the phone Saturday evening, 'so I'll have no problem keeping him occupied. But if you could limit it to half an hour so he still gets a decent time with Dad too. It's all very relaxed, though, to be honest, so when they open up the doors, I'll just leave him playing while you go in

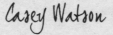

to see Jack – he loves the toys there so he might not even notice.'

I wasn't sure about that. Ethan was already getting over-excited. He couldn't get his head round quite what the connection meant. It just made him feel good that we loved his daddy too, and, bless him, I understood what he meant.

'Daddy's going to be super-excited that you found him after all this time,' he said as I helped dress him the following morning. 'He won't believe his eyes! Do you think he'll remember you?'

'Well, he'll probably notice we've got a bit more wrinkly. But yes, I think he will. At least, I hope so.'

'And will you tell him about living in your house?'

'In our house?'

Ethan nodded vigorously. 'When he leaves the big house. That he can come and live with us here. Will you tell him?'

I groaned inwardly, dismayed by the resurgence of this train of thought. Something Ethan had obviously confected for himself, as, despite my gently telling him otherwise a couple of weeks back, being the most logical thing in the world.

I would obviously need to be careful not to rein-force it. 'Um, sweetie, Daddy is a big man now, not a little boy anymore, so he doesn't need to live with me and Mike. He's going to get his own big house, remember, like I told you? And he will have a little bedroom all set up for when you go to stay with him for sleepovers. A bedroom just for you. Won't *that* be exciting?'

He considered this for a moment, thankfully seeming happy enough to revisit his plans. 'Oh,' he said, 'so will he have a bedroom for you too, like, for when you and Mike come to us for sleepovers?'

It felt as if my heart was beginning to break now, bit by little bit. The innocence of a child this young, and their simplistic thoughts – these were things that always knocked me for six. There were only minutes left before Heather turned up and the last thing I wanted to do now was upset him by reinforcing that he was going to live not with his dad but with his grandparents. Instead, I knelt down and gave him a hug.

'Wherever you live, sweetie, you can be sure that I will definitely come to visit, but I'm not sure about a sleepover. Remember I told you about Mike? The way he snores like a big elephant, and has a trumpy bum too? Ugh! Smelly bum! We can't have him sleeping over, can we?'

As I'd hoped and expected, this sent Ethan into fits of laughter, as anything to do with that part of the anatomy always did – and not just with Ethan. With most little boys of a certain age. And thankfully, for now at least, the subject was avoided. And just in time, as I then heard the doorbell. I scooted Ethan down the stairs and into the hall, where Mike had just opened the door to Heather.

'Guess what, Heather?' Ethan yelled as he skipped outside. 'Mike has a smelly bum, and he trumps. *And* he snores like an elephant!'

Mike gave me a 'What the hell?' look as he grabbed his coat from the hook. I grinned at him and passed him his car keys.

'Kids, eh?' I said, winking at Heather. 'They come out with all sorts, don't they?'

The long trip to the prison was mostly spent listening to my favourite radio station, trying to distract myself from chewing over all the thoughts and anxieties that were jockeying for position in my mind. I kept trying to reassure myself – hadn't Ethan done enough to reassure me? He adored his dad, clearly, and loved going to see him and everything pointed to the fact that Justin did too. So there were good things happening right before my eyes. I was also feeling positive about school going forwards. I was bound to be immersed in my worries on the grandparent and father front, but I needed to remember the progress being made with Ethan himself. He'd done a whole Tuesday to Friday now without a single outburst or incident (not that was relayed to me, anyway), so the school were clearly being as good as their word.

In fact, the only 'incident' so far had involved me – as in my spotting Charlie's mum, whose name I had yet to find out, edging her son away from Ethan when she picked him up from school on the Thursday afternoon. It was such a tiny thing, a small 'come away' gesture, no more, but it was sufficient to propel me in her general direction, as I could read it, and her, like a book. She'd obviously heard about the fish incident, and though I understood how terrible a thing it must have sounded, if there was one small thing I could do for Ethan, same as any child who'd suffered as he had, it would at least be to make her think. No, it might not mean that she'd see Ethan as someone she now wanted her own five-year-old to hang out with, but giving pause for thought about *why* a five-year-old would do what Ethan had was at least one step along the road of not writing him off, and similarly instilling compassion in her own child.

So I'd breezed across the road, gone straight up and said hello, and gushed straight on about how lovely it was to have Ethan back in school, and how, after the horrible circumstances of his mother's untimely death, and his distressing 'cry for help', I was *so* thrilled to see him finding a better way through that distress, and *such* a lovely friend in her Charlie. She probably thought I was bonkers, but it felt right and good. And who knew, maybe next week we could invite Charlie over on a play date. Anything not to 'monsterise' Ethan.

It felt good still. But, inevitably, as the miles rolled on by, and the sat nav counted down the minutes to our destination, I kept coming back to thoughts of Justin. He'd disappeared. He'd changed his name. He had – no getting around it – been arrested for violent assault on his former girlfriend. Seeing him through the eyes with which the Baineses clearly saw him – in essence, a monster too – was something I had to let myself do. And doing so wasn't very edifying. Were I them, would I feel any differently? It was okay him seeing Ethan in the controlled environment of a prison visit, but how could anyone currently responsible for Ethan's safety and well-being not have a responsibility to consider that past when making plans for the future? I was also anxious about what sort of reception we'd get from Justin himself. Though we'd not had it confirmed, Justin clearly knew it was us fostering Ethan; and perhaps had known that from Ethan's first visit after he'd come to us, as it was almost certainly the case that he'd have asked Ethan, and possibly Heather too, about who was caring for him. And perhaps had I asked Heather if he knew our name, she'd have confirmed it. But perhaps Justin, even if he did know, had decided not to say anything to either of them. And if so, why? I couldn't help but revisit the possibility that Justin felt we'd let him down, abandoned him. I said as much to Mike again.

'Oh, Casey,' Mike said, turning off the motorway – we weren't that far away now. 'It's Justin! Why on earth would you think that? You know as well as I do that he'll be happy we're caring for Ethan. You know, above all, that he'll be pleased to see us. Now, other than that, he will be wondering – just like we are – about how things got to where they are, and what might happen next. Now stop stressing and just relax, will you?'

I Want My Daddy

Trouble was, I found that hard to do. I had never mentioned it to Mike, because I knew what his reaction would be, but I still carried guilt about Justin moving on from us. He'd been our first ever foster child, straight after our intense period of training, in what was back then (the programme no longer exists, sadly) a specialist kind of fostering for the most challenging and troubled children; ones who had, in some cases, already been fostered, and had been deemed too difficult to care for in that setting. In short, we were a stepping stone, or a lifeline, if you like; our role was to take on these extremely challenging placements and, through a behavioural psychology-based programme of interventions, help them manage their emotions and, as a consequence, their behaviours, so they could fit more easily into a regular foster family. For some of these children, it really was a last-chance saloon. If they couldn't adapt they would end up in the less-than-ideal circumstance of a children's home or, sometimes, if they were very violent and a threat to themselves and others, a secure residential facility.

The latter had, in fact, happened, with a couple of our children and, in those cases, it was, we felt, the right outcome. One lad we had, latterly diagnosed as autistic, was actually much happier in residential care, where every aspect of his life was predictable and controlled. Another child, a girl with deep-rooted psychological problems, and whose mother had died after falling down the stairs – possibly pushed *by* her – could not be placed ultimately in a family setting, as she was too much of a suicide risk.

Justin, however, was just a deeply troubled child who, following the trauma of his very early childhood, had spent six years bouncing around in care. No one, it seemed, knew what to do with him next, so, for us, newly trained, it felt like a considerable responsibility. So, we were naturally thrilled when, after around a year with us, Justin had sufficient emotional stability to move in with his permanent foster parents, a childless couple who'd previously fostered a young lad from ten to eighteen and were now keen to do the same thing again, with another lad in need of a chance.

Yet when that placement broke down, two years after Justin went to live with them, I kept asking myself the same question: why hadn't *we* just kept him? The reasons were many and completely reasonable, and very practical. I'd just been blessed with my first grandchild and wanted to support my daughter. Kieron was still a teenager, and working hard to find ways to overcome his own challenges with Asperger's syndrome. We had trained to do a job to help multiple children. And most of all, our then supervising social worker, John Fulshaw, had explained (at the time rightly) that Justin was so emotionally damaged, and had been damaged so very young, that he'd never really be able to form close bonds with other people, us included, however much we might wish it were so.

So it had been the right thing to do, and there was no

question that Justin left us very happy to move on to his new 'forever' family. And when he later ended up in a children's home, he still kept in touch with us, and had seemed largely happy and comfortable with the environment he was then in.

But when Tyler came to stay with us, several placements down the line, that guilt couldn't help but resurface, especially when we decided we could not let Ty go. And, again, at the time, it just felt right. And not least because both Mike and I felt, and incredibly strongly, that *we* were the forever family Tyler needed. Like Ethan, Ty's mum had died of a heroin overdose. He'd been three and was found curled up next to her body. That had been years earlier – he'd been eleven when he'd come to us – and since then he'd been living with his father and stepmother, who had been reluctant to take him in, to say the least. And that stepmother, it transpired in court, had treated him very cruelly for years.

No surprise, then, that Ty had asked me, almost from the outset of the placement, 'Will you be my new mummy?' and, as the weeks passed, I'd grown increasingly sure that it was something I wanted to be too, I just had such a powerful bond with him. It was, as they say, a complete no-brainer with Ty. He loved us, we loved him, so what else would we do?

It probably helped that our own situation was, by then, very different. My kids were all grown up, and living happily with their partners, and though I had increased the grandchildren quotient by then, I could devote time to Tyler and still take in other foster kids – something he became a big part of too, both because I considered his needs before accepting any placement, and because he was now part of the family every new child came into, and was, as he grew older, a huge part of their lives, even if they were only with us for a while, just as Kieron had once been with Justin.

So, it wasn't at all the same as the circumstances had been with Justin. A very different child, and a different situation. But, now, knowing we were just about to visit Justin in prison, I couldn't help but ask myself, 'What if?'

Justin/Jack was serving his time in a big, sprawling prison set in the middle of what looked like miles and miles of open countryside and farmland. Given the time of year, most of the fields were striped brown from a recent ploughing, with next year's crops newly planted or about to be. Clouds of birds rose and fell as we passed.

I knew from Heather that Justin had gone in as a Category C prisoner but that now, with less than a year left to serve, he'd been moved to the 'open' wing of the prison, where, with good behaviour, prisoners were allowed to wear their clothes and were generally subject to fewer rules and restrictions. In some cases, they would also be able to get a job locally and for those with spouses and kids, or other relatives to put them up, would even be able to go on weekend leave. It was all part of the process of rehabilitation in readiness for their release.

Justin/Jack was apparently not in this kind of situation, having lost his rented flat when he went inside and, sadly, having no family to go to. But he did already have a parole officer, apparently, who would help him secure a job for his release, something that would be key, I knew, if he was going to get himself set up to be a part of Ethan's life.

Mike navigated the car through the big electric prison gates and made for a car-parking space, and it was only when he said, 'Earth to Casey? *Hello?* Shall I go for this one?' slightly sharply that I realised it was his second time of asking.

'Sorry, love,' I said. 'Yes, that'll be fine. Sorry, I was miles away. God, I'm so anxious about seeing him. It's crazy! I just can't stop worrying he'll think we've let him down.'

Mike parked the car and turned off the engine.

'Love,' he said gently, unbuckling his seatbelt, 'stop it. We have not let him down. *You* have not let him down. Like every other kid who's spent a night in our house, he has always known we will always be there for him. Some take it up, and some don't, and that's the way it's always been. Love, there's *no way* that Justin would be disappointed in you. Somewhere down the line he made a choice. He decided for whatever reason that he no longer needed us, but that was *his* choice to make, and not yours.' He looked past me then, out of the car window. 'Ah, there's Ethan and Heather parking up. C'mon. Let's just get out of the car, go and do what we've come to do, and let *Justin* tell us where he's at. Can we do that?'

A long speech for Mike! I felt immeasurably better. Sometimes, I just needed telling. I smiled at him and nodded. 'Sorry, love, I'm just stressed out. You know what I'm like. But yes, you're right. Let's go in and see our boy.'

As Heather had predicted, once we got through security, Ethan made straight for the play area. 'There's another one in the actual family visiting room,' she explained, 'but this one's bigger, and there's always a load of children here, waiting with family who have different visiting times or whatever, so he prefers this one. Honestly, when they call out Jack's name, you guys just go on through. He'll probably not even notice you've gone. I'll explain what's happening to the warders and we'll see you in about half an hour.'

So that's what we did. It was like going through airport security, except that I had to leave my handbag in a locker before we were allowed through, and by the time we were directed to the family visiting room I was, ridiculously, shaking like a leaf.

But isn't life funny? The very moment I saw Justin stand up to greet us, my nerves completely disappeared. What on earth had I got myself in such a state for? For here he was, such a big man now, so capable and strong-looking, yet all I saw was the lopsided grin of that eleven-year-old – a grin I'd worked so damned hard, over weeks, to coax out of that angry little face. He held out his arms, and, my eyes pricking, I ran into them.

Despite my promising Mike a thousand times that I wouldn't say anything I shouldn't, what were my first words?

'Oh, Justin! You silly lad. How did you get yourself in here?'

Time being short, we all sat down, and he told me.

Chapter 22

Justin had become Jack on his first day at work as assistant groundsman at a large stately home six years earlier. The change of identity wasn't just on a whim. In recent months Justin, then a community gardener working for the council, had got in with the wrong crowd, and in a bigger way than he ever had before, and got himself involved in drugs and heavy drinking. He had soon spiralled out of control, and by the time he realised he was going down the same route his birth mother had, it was too late to get himself out; he had run up a large debt with a drug dealer on his estate, and had found himself with a target on his back. Terrified, he did the only thing he could think of. Left his job, got a new one far enough away that he could breathe and, belt and braces, made it known on his first day at work that his birth name wasn't the one he wanted to be known as: he was generally known, he told them, as Jack.

Jack loved his new job from the get-go. He loved his new, rural surroundings, the big wide-open skies and the sense of being in another, kinder, world. Better still was the fact that the estate included workers' accommodation, and he was able to secure a small flat on the edge of the grounds. So though the wages were modest, his needs were as well, and as the fears of his old life catching up with him began receding, he wondered why it had never occurred to him to apply for this kind of work before.

Best of all, though, a few months later, he met Brogan. A new recruit in the offices, she completely beguiled him. She was beautiful, smart and seemed always to be smiling. And to his astonishment, she seemed to like him too. It almost felt as if destiny had brought him to this place, and he was determined that Brogan would be part of his future.

Within weeks the couple had started seeing each other regularly, first during Jack's breaks and then later, on dates, during one of which they both realised they'd fallen in love. And a couple of months later Brogan left her parents to move in with Jack and, rather than stay in the flat on the estate grounds, they rented a small terraced cottage in the village just around the corner from the estate.

The relationship, however, was volatile from the outset, wholly due to the fact that Jack could never quite believe his luck and was convinced Brogan would leave him at any moment. How could she not, once she

realised she was way out of his league and started listening to the parents who, from the minute they'd moved
in together, kept pointing out to her that she was much
too good for him?

The relationship, sadly, continued to spiral downhill,
weighed down by Jack's exhausting insecurity. No
matter how many times Brogan reassured Jack that she
loved him, he would always be overcome by jealousy
whenever he saw her speaking with other men at work,
and, more often than not, an argument would break
out. Eventually, what Jack feared most – rejection –
came true, following an incident which had escalated to
blows being traded, after he had wrongly accused
a workmate of chatting Brogan up. Horrified, and
sick of being treated like a possession, Brogan could
take no more. She ended the relationship and asked him
to leave.

With that rejection had come an unexpected sense of
release. His worst fears realised, they no longer had the
power to distress him. Jack had spent his entire life
coping with rejection and now, just as at every other
time in his life, he accepted it as no more than his due.
So, he found another job, worked out his notice, and,
two weeks after Brogan had, albeit gently, given him his
marching orders, packed up his few things and headed
fifty miles north. Another stately home. Another job as
an assistant groundsman.

Once again Jack tried to start a new life and this time
he made something of a success of it. He was by now

completely off-grid in terms of social media and though for a few months he and Brogan had kept in touch (she still felt sorry for him), he'd sworn off girls and was content with the life he now led; with friends who weren't too close, and a largely outdoor life, thriving on the hard physical work.

Jack did, several times, think about contacting Mike and Casey. Not because he was in trouble, but precisely because he wasn't. He'd been doing okay the last time they'd got together and a part of him felt a pull to let them know he was again. (The thought of contacting them when in the mire with the drug dealers had never once entered his head. He didn't want to *be* that person to them, the one who always messed up. Quite the opposite. He wanted them to be proud of him.) But though he was tempted, Jack didn't get in touch. He was still much too paranoid about having an online presence and, since he'd had to dump a phone when he was in the major spot of bother, so had lost Casey's number, social media would have been the only way. No matter. He'd give it time. It could wait. And in the meantime he would be the best groundsman he could be.

Eighteen months later, however, fate intervened in the shape of a text out of the blue from a former work-mate, Ivan, who'd just got engaged and was throwing a party. Would Jack like to come? They all missed him, apparently, and it would be great for him to catch up with the crew. He also added that Brogan had left the firm yonks back, so there was no worry about any awkward encounters.

Touched to have been invited, Jack booked a B and B for the night and travelled down for the reunion. Then after an afternoon catching up and a couple of hours partying, he got it into his head that he should, since he was close by, perhaps catch up with Brogan as well. After all, they hadn't exactly parted acrimoniously. He just hadn't been the one for her (he had long since accepted this) and that was an end to it. No hard feelings.

By now, however, Jack had a quantity of cider on board, something he would later acknowledge had something to do with his uncharacteristic desire to shoot the breeze with the girl who'd kicked him out. With the benefit of hindsight, he realised what he actually wanted was much the same thing as he hankered after with Mike and Casey – he wanted to show up and let her know he was doing alright. He was, he knew, just seeking approval.

Jack knew where Brogan lived because she'd told him at the time. It hadn't been much after that that she'd stopped getting in touch and, Jack being Jack – or more pertinently, Justin being Justin – there was no way he'd have got in touch with her. Now, though, in the area, and with an itch that wanted scratching, he made his way on foot, albeit a little unsteadily, to the address that was stored in his phone.

The house was completely dark, no lights coming from any windows, and though Jack knocked several times, he wasn't hopeful. He was just about to leave when he heard that familiar voice.

'*Jack*? Jack, is that you?' It was Brogan, and she was slurring her words. Even in his slightly inebriated state he knew right away that she was worse. She was talking to him from the front path of the house next door, from which she had obviously just emerged. 'Oh my God, it *is* you!' she said 'Fucking hell!' Then, coming round to her own path, having fumbled with the gate latch, said, 'I'll just find my keys. We can have a drink, can't we? Fucking hell, Jack, I can't believe it's you!'

Jack, though far from sober, still had a keen nose for a very bad idea. As she drew level with him, rummaging in her bag for her door keys, he decided then and there that he would not. 'You're alright,' he said. 'I can see you've had a few. I just thought I'd stop by and –'

'Yes, I have. And you know what? We'll have a few more, eh?' she said, stabbing at the keyhole with the door key.

He took the key from her and unlocked the door. 'You're alright,' he said again. But then changed his mind. He badly needed a pee, and could at least see her in safely.

It was the decision that would become his undoing. As soon as he stepped into the hallway he was appalled. Brogan had kept their cottage as neat as a pin, but this place was, to put it mildly, a tip. It not only looked dirty, it smelled dirty too. And messy, every horizontal surface cluttered with mess and dirty crockery, including the floor. And something else. All around were kids' toys. He turned to her and, seeing her inane, unfocussed grin, realised that whatever she was high on, it wasn't just booze. He's been around drugs enough to know. What had happened to her? He spread his hands. 'You have a *kid* now?'

'Indeed I do,' she said, giggling. Then put a finger to her lips. 'Shh now, or you'll wake him.'

Jack gaped. 'He's here? And you were ...'

'Oh, get over yourself, will you? I'm only next door. And he's *asleep*. In his cot. What's your problem?'

A cot. He did some maths. 'A baby? You left a *baby*?'

'He's not a baby,' she retorted. 'He's *three*. What's your problem? It's not like –'

'He's *three*?' Cogs began whirring now. 'Whose is he?'

Brogan laughed a thin laugh at him. '*Durrr*. Whose do you think?'

It had been a long time, a long time indeed, since the rage hit. A long time since he'd even revisited the memories, because he'd learned to block them out a long time ago. Some psychologist, once, had told him that was good and right and normal. Your brain does this great job of protecting you from harm, she'd said. It knows which corners of your memory it's best not to take you to.

But he was there now. In that stinking bedroom, his brothers wet and soiled and howling. And no nappies. No food. No nothing for any of them. Just dog fucking food for his mother's fucking dog, who, like her, wasn't there, never was. Because *she* was never fucking there. Not when it got dark and she got bored and restless. Won't be long, she would say. Just popping out, she would say. You get off to bed now. I'll be back before you know it, she would say. And he'd sit there and sit there, in the cold and the dark, his brothers' cries like knives, twisting around in his empty gut.

He looked at Brogan again now, but he was seeing his mother.

Later he would tell the police, truthfully, that he had lost his mind. That he hadn't known what he was doing. That the rage and the violence that he could not deny were as if they were happening to someone else. He had no memory of holding Brogan by the throat, but he could not deny the evidence of the bruises, or the testimony of the man who had come in and found them once she'd started screaming. The man who was her neighbour, the man she did the drugs with. While her son – *his* son – was left all on his own.

Once Jack fell silent, it took a few seconds for me to compose myself. I'd known the bare bones of his encounter with Brogan, but that was obviously before I'd known it was him. Not that it made a difference; I had always been in the habit of trying not to leap to judgement, and what I knew of Jack was what I'd seen for myself: he was a dad trying to do his best to keep up a relationship with a son he loved, from prison.

But now I did know Jack was Justin, and I felt a deep sense of the sadness of it all. He was obviously, as he'd said, the architect of his own misfortune, but with my much deeper knowledge of the childhood which had shaped who he was my heart bled for him all over again.

What a mess. But there was no point looking back. It was what it was. Though something important suddenly occurred to me.

'But this was, when – almost two years ago or there-abouts? And you mean to say you've been here all this time? That seems an awfully long sentence, given the circumstances.'

'That's my fault,' he said. 'I'd have been out eighteen months ago but I just couldn't cope, Casey. Not once I realised what I'd done, and the fact that I'd never even met the boy, and had let him down already. And knowing I'd likely never see him again … well, I just wanted to die. I set fire to my cell, hoping to kill myself, because I just couldn't live with all that guilt. And when that didn't work, I was in such a state … was just so angry at everything that I wanted to fight anyone and everyone.' He shook his head and sighed. 'I got myself into some real bother here – I didn't realise you didn't know that – and next thing I knew, I was right back in court and had another year slapped onto my sentence.'

'Jesus, mate!' Mike said, with feeling. 'But fair play to you – looks like you had a change of heart at least. I mean, look at you. You're still here to tell the tale.' He reached across and touched Justin's hand, an unexpectedly tender gesture. 'It's so good to see you, mate,' he said. 'I can't tell you. Eh, and when did you know, you know, that it was us looking after your Ethan?'

That touched me too. That Mike automatically said 'your Ethan'.

It made Justin smile. 'Right away,' he said. 'The first time he visited once he was with you. I'd been so … well, so upset. About Brogan. About what might be going to happen. I was braced for a fight. I didn't know if her parents would come forward. To be honest, my biggest fear was that they might put him up for adoption. Took a bit for me to be convinced they really couldn't. That he was being fostered and that I could go on seeing him just as always. That reassured me a *lot*. And I found out it was you because I asked Ethan, didn't I? I wanted to know who he was with, how they were treating him and that. And there can't be many Caseys doing fostering round your way, can there? I asked, though, just to check. Said was she this high' – he stuck a hand out – 'with black hair?'

We all laughed at that. 'And I should have known sooner than I did,' I responded. 'When Ethan asked me for spaghetti bollock naked. Tell me, though, why didn't you say that you knew us?'

His expression briefly darkened. 'Because I didn't know what might happen. I worried they'd take him off you and maybe put him somewhere else. So, when I got the visit request, I was well happy. Though Bob said I shouldn't have worried, because it was never a problem anyway.'

'Bob?' Mike asked.

'The prison counsellor. They got me hooked up with him as soon as I was put on suicide watch, and honestly, since you two, he's the best thing that ever happened to me. Got me sorted, like, my head straight – well,' he grinned sheepishly, 'eventually. And it was thanks to him that I got to see my Ethan on a regular basis. Honestly, that man literally saved my life.'

I sent a silent prayer to Bob as I listened to Justin explain how the man had got him a solicitor, who then made all the necessary arrangements so that contact could happen. Justin had, rightly, been really worried that Ethan was already being neglected, and that if Brogan didn't get herself together, something he was powerless to control, his son's future well-being was at stake. His solicitor had obviously used Justin's testimony in court, and one positive to come out of that awful situation was that Brogan came under the radar of social services and Ethan was allocated a family support worker in the form of Heather. Thanks to those trips the relationship between father and son had grown and flourished into what it was today.

'I was devastated when I heard that Brogan had died,' Justin said sadly, 'but at the same time I wasn't too surprised. I suppose I'm lucky, really, that I didn't know how bad things had got, else I might have lost my shit all over again. I just felt so bad for my boy when I heard.

So, hearing he was with you guys was the *biggest* relief. And really helped me get my head where it needs to be now. Which is good, because I just got my release date. So long as I stay on track, I'll be out in just under four months.'

I glanced at Mike before speaking again, and then reached across to take Justin's hand. 'That's fantastic news, love,' I said. 'I'm *so* happy for you, but you know that his grandparents are going ahead with their fostering application, don't you?'

Justin nodded. He didn't seem fazed by the knowledge. 'I can't do anything about that yet, and I don't intend to, either. They may hate me, but I know they love my little boy, and they brought Brogan up, didn't they, so I know they'll do their best. To tell you the truth, Casey, although I love Ethan with all my heart, I'm not stupid. I know I can't give him what he needs right now. I have nothing, do I? When I come out I'll be starting all over again, from scratch, and he doesn't deserve to have to make that journey with me. He deserves a dad with enough sense to make sure he gets what he needs till I'm in a position to be a proper dad to him.'

I started to cry, I just couldn't help it. This was Justin at his very best. Pragmatic and selfless. 'You're a good boy, Justin,' I said, through a flurry of tears and snot, 'and I feel so, so sorry for you. You know, you could have picked up the phone at any point during all of this, and we'd have been there like a shot for you, don't you?'

I Want My Daddy

'Stop crying, Casey,' he said, smiling at me gently. 'Of course I know that, and maybe I should have, but I didn't. What I do know, though, is that I accept all that has happened and take responsibility for it. I've built a life before and I can do it again. But I swear, I will be there for Ethan. I will see him whenever I'm allowed to and I will try my best to gain Brogan's mum and dad's trust. He deserves that much from me, at the very least.'

'He does, love, and so do you,' I said. 'Now come here and give me a big hug, so we can leave and let you have some time with your boy.'

I was still sobbing on and off the whole journey home, so I was glad Ethan was travelling with Heather. But I had my answers now, and I had renewed faith in Justin. Or, rather Jack, as he gently reminded us we needed to think of him as, and call him now, just before we left him.

'Bloody balls to working on Ethan's behaviour,' I said to Mike eventually. 'We will leave that to the professionals and his teachers at school. From now on my only concern is making sure that Ethan is going to be happy living with his grannie and pops, and then helping Justin – no, *Jack* – to repair his relationship with them. That's my mission and I choose to accept it!'

Mike grinned. 'Ah, there she is,' he chortled at me. 'Glad to have you back, girl, and not that whimpering wreck I've just had to put up with for the last hour and a half.'

He got a punch for that, just to rubberstamp that I really was back. And as for that mission, I meant every word.

Chapter 23

We all knew, because it was hardly the secret of the century, that for Ethan there was only one place he wanted to move. To wherever his dad would next call home. Which was remarkable, when you thought about it. If you added up the sum total of hours they'd spent together since Jack had first found out he was Ethan's father it amounted to not very much at all. However, a part of me was relaxed about how Ethan would react when it was relayed to him that that wasn't happening. He was only five and would very soon adapt to his new reality, especially if his visits to see his dad were to continue – that being the principal goal of my mission. It was not for me to try an influence the Baineses unduly, but there was no rule that said I couldn't gently keep commenting on just how valuable Ethan's bond with his father was.

Only a few days after the visit, however, I began to get a sense of just how resistant to living with his grandparents Ethan was. He had come out from school in the foulest of moods, and refused to speak about it until we got back home.

'I want my daddy!' he yelled almost as soon as we got through the door. 'I'm not living with my grannie and pops, not *never*!'

After ten minutes of my trying to unpick where this outburst had come from, Ethan was calm enough to tell me what had happened.

'We drawed some pictures at dinner time when it rained and we couldn't play out, and I drawed my grannie an' pops, only I couldn't draw that special chair what pops has. I asked Miss to help me an' CJ laughed and laughed, an' he picked my drawing up and showed it to everyone, an' he was saying Pops is stupid 'cos he got no legs, but he *does* have legs an' I'm *not* living there, not with that stupid, stupid chair. And CJ said Pops won't never play football with me, not never, because he can't kick a ball even!'

It was such a tirade it quite took my breath away. He'd finished by folding his arms across his chest and looking at me with a 'How about *that*, then?' expression, which would have been comical if it hadn't upset him so much.

'Well, what a silly thing to say,' I said briskly. 'CJ doesn't know anything! Of course your pops can walk, he has two special sticks that help him, and that chair is way cooler than any other chairs you can sit in because it has wheels and can whizz down the street really, really fast!'

Ethan eyed me suspiciously and looked as if he were struggling to believe me, so I continued right on. 'And another thing that CJ probably doesn't know is that the guy who played Superman was in a wheelchair as well. Yes, that's right, a real live *superhero!*' I offered up an apology to the late Christopher Reeve, for my half-truth. 'And, did you know, one of the most famous scientists in the whole wide world was called Professor Stephen Hawking? And he was in a wheelchair, too, just like your pops. So, your pops is really just like those very special people.'

Which Ethan seemed to accept as suitable ammunition for the following day. Nonetheless, not five minutes after, he let out a heavy sigh. 'But *still*, Casey, why can't I live with my daddy, like all the other kids do? It's not *fair*.'

It wasn't fair, but life wasn't always fair, and I spent the rest of the week having similar conversations with Ethan, trying to convince him how life was going to be good when he went to live with his grandparents. I also got Grace, who came to do a play therapy session the following Saturday, to spend her hour working on his worries about this. And she tried her best, using techniques she usually reserved for children who were moving to a new foster placement or school.

'Same principles, different circumstances,' she said after the session. 'But he's very resistant, and I'm sure it's because the event is so close to the time that his dad will be home, and he can't see what the problem is.

Neither does he understand why he can't just stay here with you till his dad gets the fairy-tale house of his imaginings and he can skip the grandparents part altogether.'

Grace was spot on with her assessment of course, and who wouldn't be able to see his logic? The dad he knew and loved versus the two people he barely knew from Adam? But it didn't help us in the here and now, and wouldn't help with the transition.

We had a busy few weeks ahead, starting with another contact visit with Ethan's grandparents the following Friday afternoon, and then another prison visit booked for the Sunday. I decided to email Christine and ask for her help to get booked onto that next visiting order as well, because, in my gut, I knew that it would in all likelihood be Jack – and *only* Jack – that could get through to his son and get the transition off to a positive start.

'I'll get onto that straight away,' Christine said when she phoned me, 'and if it helps in any way, it's looking more and more likely that the grandparents are going to go ahead with their fostering application. Well, actually, it's a kinship arrangement, which has all the support that fostering offers, but is more laid-back – it's what we tend to use it when it's family members or close friends taking on a child. We've explained it all to them and they like the idea, but they still, sad to say, seem to be against the idea of Jack playing a role once he's released.'

'But they're happy for him to see him now?'

'They have no control over that. To be honest, I think they're just putting down their marker. If they don't feel comfortable about Jack being part of their lives, then they don't want to be bullied into accepting him. When it comes to it, they might feel differently. I hope so. And for what it's worth, I genuinely think they will.'

'Oh, I hope so too,' I said, 'but that's still sad to hear. I was hoping to have something positive to tell Jack when I go back on Sunday.'

'You can't do that, Casey,' Christine reminded me. 'That's down to Lydia, and Lydia alone. I know it's hard, but you can't involve yourself with that side of things. You have to remain very, very neutral.'

'Switzerland I shall be then,' I said. 'But it's so hard for us. Jack was like family. And I know he'll do right by Ethan. I just want Jocelyn and Alan to know the side of him that we do. What happened in *his* childhood. They'd change their minds, then. I know they would.'

'And maybe they will,' Christine said, 'but that has to be their decision, and one to make when *they* are ready. Jack will always have his rights, and, if we have anything to do with it, he *will* have regular contact, but as for happy families, well, that could be a long way off. Don't forget they still blame him for their daughter's spiral into drink and drugs. And they're recently bereaved. It's still too raw for them right now.'

I sighed as I hung up. Christine was right. Grace was right. Hell, the grandparents were right! It suddenly felt like it was me, Mike and Jack against the full weight of the system, and though I knew it was the reality, I still found it hard to bear. For now, though, I had to put that to one side. I had another contact session to support Ethan with, and then another prison visit where I'd be asking a father to tell his son that he couldn't live with him after all. Yes, I knew Jack had already accepted this as inevitable, but I also knew he probably saw this as a bit of a *fait accompli* – and hadn't realised that those words would have to come from his mouth, which would be really hard for Ethan to hear.

The plan was that I'd pick Ethan up from school on Friday, then take him to the nearby McDonald's drive-through for some food to eat in the car, before heading the short way to the contact centre.

'This is *already* the best day ever,' he explained to me, as we drove into the car park, and he was busy gathering his food wrappers to put in the bin.

'I'm very glad to hear that,' I told him.

'And if they've buyed me presents, it will be even *betterer*, won't it?'

I agreed it would be nice, but with a small necessary homily about setting up expectations and that life wasn't all about grown-ups buying you things. All of which, I knew, whooshed right over his head. Getting presents from them would of *course* be 'betterer'. Rubbish deposited, we strode up the same little path where I'd first met Mr Baines. This time, however, we were met by Lydia at the door.

She smiled at Ethan and then at me. 'Grandparents are already in the playroom,' she said, 'and, Casey, they've said that you're more than welcome to sit in if you like. Heather's already in there, making her usual contact notes, so you could sit at the back with her and just observe, if that's okay?'

It didn't really sound like a request – more like a definite instruction, and it made it all sound weirdly formal, but I nodded my assent and followed her through the corridor, Ethan still holding my hand. Despite his upbeat mood, he was clinging quite tightly, so I breathed a sigh of relief when he saw his grandparents and let go immediately so he could run across to them. A good start.

As it would be, for of course they hadn't come empty-handed. You had to do what you had to do, I thought, as I waved and took my seat, as instructed. 'You buyed me presents!' Ethan whooped as he spied the brightly wrapped gifts on his grandad's lap. 'CJ says you can't walk properly, or kick a ball and play football, but Casey says you can, and you're like Superman, only older. And like a scientist who's very famous and has no legs.' He glanced across at me for corroboration. 'That's right, isn't it?'

I burrowed down as deep as I could into my collar as I tried to recall ever mentioning that Stephen Hawking had lost his legs, but Alan Baines's laugh was as genuine as it was booming. 'She's right, lad,' he said. 'I've got a brain the size of Leeds, me, and I'll be kicking a ball about with you in no time. Can't fly, mind, but at least I'll have three feet to kick with, what with my one, and two sticks.'

So that was alright, thank goodness. Jocelyn Baines, in particular, was in stitches, and though the idea that laughter is the best medicine still has its limitations, I hoped having Ethan in their lives would help them both laugh again, after such a terrible loss.

The two-hour visit whizzed by in similar high spirits. Both Alan and Jocelyn clearly loved this little boy and Ethan was fast learning that they seemed to worship the ground he walked upon, and wasn't slow in using it to his advantage. What really surprised me, though, was how Ethan instinctively seemed to know not to talk about his daddy, and that glaring omission made me feel slightly sad. Some adults simply had no idea what an impact their own biases had on children. No wonder some kids in care became experts at manipulation – it was the adults who taught them this survival method, without even realising it. Mum doesn't like Dad, play them against each other. Nan and Grandad don't like Dad, so you never mention Dad. Dad doesn't like Nan and Grandad, tell Dad you don't want to live with them. Was this what was happening here? Was Ethan already that astute that he knew what all the adults felt about each other and was playing his part to perfection? I was determined to find out, because in my book that shouldn't happen.

At the end of the session, Lydia came back into the

room and asked me to join her and Jocelyn outside in the corridor.

'Mrs Baines was asking, Casey, if you wouldn't mind if you and she swapped phone numbers. It's been agreed that – if you're on board with it, that is – some phone or FaceTime contact can take place. Just an informal arrangement between yourselves. Would this be okay?'

'That would be brilliant,' I said. 'I'm sure Ethan will get a lot out of that, but if it's okay, can we do it really casually? As in don't push it; let Ethan take the lead on it? I just don't like setting these things in stone, as in like every Friday, or something. You know what kids are like if they're busy playing or engrossed in something, they soon start to resent having to break off. I find it's far better to just ask them now and again if they fancy a phone call.'

'Oh, of course, that's all absolutely fine!' Mrs Baines said, 'I don't want to force anything on him, just, anytime at all, just when he fancies a chat, we'd love that.'

'Perfect,' I said, reaching into my handbag for a pen and paper. I scribbled down my number and handed it over. 'If you just drop me a text when you get home, I'll save your details in my phone and then Ethan will give you a ring. Though you don't *have* to wait for that, of course. If you get the urge to chat with Ethan or you've got any concerns or questions, you're welcome to give me a call anytime you like.'

I felt buoyed and relieved as I drove home. This new and unexpected development would give me the opportunity to make friends with Jocelyn, or at least get to know her more, and then hopefully I'd get the chance to eventually talk to her about our version of Jack. About Justin. There was still a long way to go, but at least now I could see a road I could follow. I just had to be careful how I would tread that road. Christine had been crystal clear about my boundaries and I couldn't cross them. Not if I wanted to make this transition smooth for everyone involved, and that included me.

Chapter 24

As I suspected, the first FaceTime contact went really well. We didn't waste any time in fact, and I made the call to Grannie on the Saturday, the day after the last contact. Before telling Ethan, I took the phone out to the garden and started the face-to-face call with just me and Jocelyn, as I really did want to get more of a feel for her.

'It's not too early, is it?' I asked, smiling at the screen. 'Because I can call back later if that's better. I haven't said anything to Ethan yet.'

'Early risers in this house,' Jocelyn replied, laughing, 'so it's never too early. Where is he? Playing or watching *Paw Patrol*?'

'You're learning fast!' I said. 'And yes, he's doing both actually. Got it on the telly and playing with his figures on the rug. I just wanted a quick word if that's okay? I mean, I don't want there to be any awkwardness at all between us, so I wanted to make sure you knew that we are visiting Jack again tomorrow – we're going down with Ethan.'

Jocelyn's face tightened slightly, but she was still smiling. 'Yes, we're aware that you're going and it's fine. I understand that you and Mike also fostered Jack at one point. How strange all this must be for you.'

'Well, it was a bit of a shock when we found out, but yes, we fostered him a long time ago, he was our first foster child, in fact. He was called Justin then. I don't know if you knew that.'

'We did. Our daughter told us all about him.' Her smile dropped then. 'Look, Casey – is it okay that I call you Casey?' I nodded. She glanced around as if checking that no one was listening. 'I get that you have a history with Jack, and I don't want to intrude on that, but we do too, and our history with him wasn't good.' She paused for a moment and then said, 'I am working on my husband, I really am, but he is so set in his ways. That said, we both accept that Jack is part and parcel of having Ethan. We don't have to like it, and much will depend on what happens when he leaves prison, but I'm going to try to get Alan to be a bit more accepting. That's the best I can promise you right now.'

She understood my concerns, that was clear, and what was also clear was the fact that she was struggling with torn feelings, and who could blame her? Her loyalties obviously lay with her daughter, yet here she was talking about accepting Jack.

I Want My Daddy

'Thank you, Jocelyn, both for being so understanding and for being honest with me, that's all I can ask, and I promise you, I'll do the same for you. Now, I'll go get that little firecracker of a grandson for you, so you can chat.'

Her smile was back, and her face lit up as I plonked my phone in front of Ethan's face. It was heartwarming to watch him jumping up and down and pointing the screen towards the TV to show Grannie his programme, and kind of amazing, too. This child and this woman barely knew each other, after all. Both were taking that massive leap of faith in moving forward as one family now.

I left them to it, asking Ethan to bring my phone back when he said goodbye. Mike had gone in to work for a half day, so I busied myself in the kitchen while they chatted. I felt quite uplifted after having spoken so candidly with Jocelyn, who I reckoned was a woman with a fair bit of wisdom. And though I'd hated feeling like the piggy in the middle, I supposed that's exactly what I was, really. Saying that, however, I'd always prided myself on being very good at building bridges between feuding families, and that's exactly what I intended to do with this very broken one.

My next job was to work on Jack. I knew he felt pushed aside by the Baines family, and resented the fact that they'd all kept Ethan's very existence away from him until he had found out himself, accidentally, but still, he'd already accepted that they could give Ethan a good life, so it wasn't too much of a stretch to ask him to get Ethan to believe that too, not just see it as something he must endure.

The same as the previous week, Mike and I travelled to the prison in Mike's car, while Ethan went with Heather in hers. Jack had asked that we all go in together this time so we could see him with his son, and we were happy to do that, but I hoped that I'd get the opportunity to speak to Jack by himself.

'We'll just stay for an hour,' I told Mike as we made our way to the entrance, 'but if Heather doesn't take Ethan off to play for a bit, can you do it? I just want to try again with Jack. You know, about the grandparents.'

Mike sighed. 'Okay, but don't go overboard, Case. Remember what Christine said, stay neutral.'

Bloody neutral! Like that was an option in this case. Two warring parties and a child trying to please both. This wasn't a time for taking sides or staying put. It was a situation that demanded I take some kind of action, even if as subtly as possible. (I take ownership of most of my faults, and my lack of ability to be subtle is one of them, unfortunately.)

'Switzerland!' I reminded Mike. 'I promise. In fact, I couldn't be more Switzerland if I donned a pair of lederhosen and started singing the bloody "Lonely Goatherd"!'

If it had been wonderful to see Justin – no, Jack – again, it was even more gratifying to see father and son together. To really see the result of their shared DNA, those little idiosyncrasies, that similarity in their features. Ethan had done him another painting. No houses, big or small. Just Chase and the gang and some important shapes and squiggles, and to see him explaining to Jack what they were was as touching a scene as I'd seen in a long time, so tender – and *normal* – was the moment between them. I sat back and drank it in, happy just to watch them interacting, so glad to see their undeniable bond for myself. But the time had to come, then, for me to add my sixpence worth into the current situation so, duly nudged by me, Mike suggested he and Heather take Ethan for a run-around in the play area after the long journey in the car, while Jack and I discussed some bits and bobs.

I wasted no time getting to the point, pointing out to Jack how resistant Ethan was to living with Grannie Jo and Pops, and how, though he wasn't going to have a choice in the matter, it would be so much easier for him if he had his dad's blessing and, more than that, that he heard it from his own lips.

He listened intently, then looked at me, frowning. 'Casey, those people absolutely despise me,' he said. 'If it had been up to them I would never have known I had a son, and you want me to tell him that I *want* him to go live with them, that I can't have him with me, and that's that?'

I hadn't thought of that aspect of things. That they'd not given a thought to their daughter's child's father, when Brogan was pregnant, and what *he* might have wished for his unborn child. Still, that was then and this was now, and if Ethan was to settle happily with his grandparents, those bridges needed building. 'Well, yes, basically. Don't forget I've been getting to know Ethan a lot over these past weeks and I see what he's doing. He feels torn, love, like he's being a traitor to you if he likes them, and then when he's with them he feels the same in reverse. It's not right and it's not good for his emotional well-being.'

'So, you're saying that to make him happy, all he needs is my blessing? I'm sorry, Casey, but I don't believe that. He barely knows them! When Brogan was alive I used to phone her after Ethan's visits to see me, and she'd tell me how they never once helped her out, and that they didn't even *care* that she had a kid.'

This too was new, but obviously not the whole story. And of course Brogan, so angry with the parents she'd become estranged from, would paint them in a bad light to Jack. I sighed and tried to explain that it was *because* they cared that they had been so harsh with her. 'Tough love, love,' I said to Jack. 'Remember us talking about that? Boundaries? They knew she was doing drink and drugs and hoped that, by refusing to help her out financially, Brogan would realise how much she needed them, and might go back home, or might at least stop getting in over her head. It wasn't that they didn't love her, *or* Ethan. It was precisely because they loved them that they tried to make her see sense. And I don't think it's true that they didn't try. I think Brogan's mum tried pretty hard, and for a pretty long time. But look what she was up against …'

'What?'

'What do you think, love? Drug addiction. And addicts will sell their soul for their next fix, and rebuff anyone who tries to stop them. You know as well as I do that drug use distorts everything. What Brogan told you was not the whole story.'

He shook his head. 'But they didn't try hard *enough*,' Jack said, his face sad now. 'And Brogan was doing what I'd always done with my mother. Reaching out, and when they knocked her back and refused to support her, she acted out and got worse. Eventually, you just cut them off to save the pain.'

'Oh, Jack,' I said, reaching to hold his hand. 'I do see that, and I'm sorry, love. And you know, they *are* sorry now. More sorry than perhaps you can imagine; they know they handled things badly, and they'll never have the chance to make it right now, either. Can you imagine how terrible that must feel? But they're determined to love Ethan and never, ever let him down. They'll see that in you too, eventually, I know it, but, love, it was their daughter. It's still unimaginably painful for them, but they want to do the right thing. I know they do.'

I could see unshed tears beginning to glint in Jack's eyes as he looked over at Ethan, busy building some structure with bright, plastic bricks, and laughing with Heather and Mike.

'I'll do it,' he said eventually, 'but I'm scared he'll hate me, Casey. I've been weak, I know I have. He always talks about when we'll live together, and I've never properly corrected him because one day we will, and that's a *definite*.'

'I know, love, but he has to know that time isn't yet, and if it's to work like it should, then it's *got* to come from you. If it comes from someone else, he'll expect you to fight it. Fight for *him*. And when you don't, because you can't – we all know that's true for now – how will that make you look and feel?' I squeezed his hand. 'I promise you, Jack,' I said, desperately hoping that I was right, 'he won't hate you for doing this. Far from it. It will release him from feeling he has to pick a side. Yes, he might test you, and get upset, but he *will* get over it, get used to it, and, as time goes by, he'll know you did it because of how much you love him and want the very best for him. And hey, who knows what the future holds? In time I know that you'll have a better relationship with the Baineses and, from that, a completely different future for you and Ethan might emerge.'

'Will you stay here, Casey? You and Mike, while I tell him? It's just, I might not be able to hack it and have to leave.'

'Of course we will,' I said, 'but you *will* hack it, Jack, you'll do it for him.' I pointed towards Ethan, who noticed and decided he now wanted to run across to us. 'No time like the present,' I said as I gave his hand a final squeeze before letting go.

'Come here, big man,' Jack said as he swung Ethan up and onto his knee. He then looked at Heather and smiled, 'I don't suppose you could go for a coffee, could you? I just need a word with my little fellow.'

'My treat,' Mike said. 'I'll nip off too. I could do with stretching my own legs after being knelt down on those mats.'

'You like Casey, Daddy?' Ethan asked a little nervously, causing me to arch my brows at Jack. This kid was a watcher of human behaviour, for sure.

'Of course I do,' Jack laughed. 'We both love Casey, don't we?' He tickled Ethan's sides, causing him to double up laughing. 'And guess who else we love?'

'Mike?'

'Well, yes, but you know who I love too?'

'Who, Daddy?'

'Grannie Jo of course, and Pops. We love them too, don't we?'

Ethan stopped laughing and stared hard at Jack. 'Um, a little bit,' he agreed, after a moment of reflection. 'Pops is funny. They buy me presents. Do you know them too, then? I didn't know'd that. I thought they were shitbags. Mummy always said they were.'

He was actively searching Jack's eyes as though looking for clues to check if this was real, or a trick. I was struck too by the way it all rolled off his tongue as one. Funny. Buying presents. Also shitbags – just another word to him. Because that's what Mummy had drilled into him about them for all of his short life, like A is for Apple. Just another fact to be absorbed.

It occurred to me how compartmentalised Ethan's life was now. On the one hand, his beloved daddy, on the other, his maternal grandparents. That a relationship might exist between them had never even occurred to him. Why would it? His sense of what a family might look like was now having to be completely reshaped.

'Course it's okay, son. They love you like mad – almost as much as I do, which is a *lot*. So yes, I do know them – they are your mummy's mummy and daddy. And yes, I do love them. Mostly because of how much they love *you*. And I want you to know that I'm really happy that you're going to go live with them. It's going to be so much fun for you, and when I leave this place, I'll get to see you loads, 'cos you'll be right there at Grannie and Pops' place, where I can come see you.'

Ethan's eyes filled with tears. He reached up a hand to stroke Jack's face, almost as if confirming he was real. 'But … but what about me an' you, Daddy, and us going to live in our big house? Hey, Daddy, what about *you*? Where will *you* live?'

Jack tried his best, but couldn't hold it together. The tears fell onto his cheeks and he made no move to wipe them. I could tell he was struggling to speak now. 'I can't do this,' he said eventually, to no one in particular. He cleared his throat. 'I'm sorry, little mate,' he said, kissing Ethan's forehead. 'But Daddy has a bad tummy ache and needs to go to bed. But you be good for Casey and Mike till our next visit, okay? And remember what I said about Grannie and Pops, mate. I love them, and I want you to love them too. And to go and live with them, son, so they can look after you till we can properly be together. You hear me? And you mustn't' – his voice was cracking now – 'worry about me.'

He passed Ethan, really crying now, to sit instead on my knee, then walked away, signalling for a guard to allow him out of the room. He didn't look back again, not once. It was wretched to watch and I felt terrible. I'd practically forced Jack to put himself through that, and now both he and Ethan were inconsolable, but as we walked out of that prison and I told Heather that Ethan would travel back with us, I was still sure that I'd done the right thing. Yes, it had been horrible for both of them, but Ethan needed to know that it was okay for him to share his love. He deserved to be free to do this without feeling guilty, and Jack had taken the first step in allowing him to do so.

The trusted iPad kept Ethan's mind off things for most of the long journey home, but eventually he did ask a couple of questions, as if he were trying now to process what had happened.

'Will Daddy be okay now, Casey? His tummy must have really hurt.'

'Daddy will be fine now,' I said. 'In fact, I bet he's putting that picture up that you drew for him. I bet that's exactly what he's doing.'

'It's a good picture,' he said. 'It will make him feel better.'

'Exactly,' I said.

A moment passed. Then, 'Can Daddy come and live with Grannie and Pops when he leaves his big house? Can you ask them?'

'No, sweetheart,' I said, 'because Daddy is a grown-up, remember, so he's going to get his own grown-up place, where you will be able to go and visit him.'

'But he could, though, if he wanted to,' he persisted.

'Well, yes, that's true,' I rattled on, winging it now, aware of Mike's amused half-smile, 'but, you know, Daddy likes completely different programmes to Grannie and Pops, and likes doing his keep fit in the living room, things like that, and making his own spaghetti bollock-naked late at night sometimes, and everything, so it's not sensible for him to live with them because they'd all be under each other's feet.'

I waited to see if he'd absorb and accept this. Which, thankfully, he seemed to. Mike, meanwhile, was really struggling not to laugh out loud. 'But will they still buy presents for him?' Ethan went on. 'If people love people they buy them presents a lot, don't they?'

'You know, I don't actually know,' I said. 'But perhaps they will, for Christmas. And you know what I do know, for certain? That they'll help you choose a lovely gift for *you* to give Daddy. What d'you think he might like for Christmas? It's not so far away now, after all.'

Mike grunted theatrically. 'Oh, cripes,' he groaned. '*Please* don't remind me.'

'I think he'd like a *Paw Patrol* T-shirt,' Ethan said firmly.

'Oh, yes,' I said. 'Now that is one *brilliant* idea. You'll have fun going shopping for that with Grannie Jo, for sure.'

'And one for Pops, too,' he said. 'So he doesn't feel left out.'

I twisted around. Ethan was smiling to himself, totally unaware that it was *him* who was going to be the best Christmas present this year. For all of them.

He looked up at me then, iPad timer at the ready. 'How long till we're home? Is it twenty or thirty or fifty or sixty?' He grinned cheekily. 'Or is "round about" or "soon"?'

'Soon,' I said. And God willing, it would be.

Epilogue

Dear Casey & Mike

I hope you're both well and had a lovely Christmas and New Year. Silly me, of course you did, in fact I bet the house looked like Santa's grotto from November! (I can imagine you running around like a loony all day, and Mike sitting with his Guinness, rolling his eyes. Am I right? :)) I just wanted to write to let you know how thankful I am for everything you did for my boy, and for me too. I'm not just talking about when I was a kid, I mean for all you've done for me just lately, getting me to be sensible for Ethan's sake, and making his move that much easier for me – and him! – to cope with.

You might not know this, but I've been writing letters to Jocelyn and Alan for the past few weeks – almost every day! And two weeks ago they both wrote me back. I couldn't believe my eyes when the warden brought me my mail and I saw the postmark. I didn't even dare to open it till teatime, and even then I had to get my mate to read it out to me. You'll never guess what they wanted, but I'll tell you, haha, they wanted to know if Jocelyn could come see me with Ethan!

Oh, Casey, I was so nervous, but I'm so pleased we did it, it was a really good day. While Ethan played, we talked about Brogan, about how I had been with her, and then we talked about Ethan and how much her and Alan love him. I swear down, I never slagged Brogan off once, because they don't deserve that, do they? Anyway, it's looking good so far, Jocelyn seems to have forgiven me for my part and she says that Alan has softened as well. Apparently, Ethan is always talking about me to his grandad and Jocelyn said that Alan told her that I can't be that bad if the kid thinks so highly of me. :)

Oh, the other good news is that I've been told my release date is 1 March if I continue to behave myself and keep my head down. I swear I've never tried so hard! I've been doing a farming course and I get to go out to work every day and transport collects me on a morning and brings me back at 6.00 p.m. I love it, even better than gardening, haha. Who would have thought, me milking cows LOL! But anyway, Jocelyn knows my release date now as I've been using my phone allowances to call her and speak with Ethan, which is ace, and she's said not to worry, that her and Alan are looking forward to it, and basically they are saying I can have as much contact as I want if I stay on the right tracks, which I will do. She's even told the judge at the hearing that she's open to 'free contact' and they told her if anything changes, she can get a solicitor and take it back to court, but I'm determined not to mess up, Casey, this is the biggest chance I'm ever going to get.

Right, I'll get off now because I'm not much of a writer – it makes my fingers hurt LOL :) but give my love to everyone – oh, and I hope the wedding was the best day ever for you all, say hi to everyone, specially the happy couple! Hopefully, we can all meet up in the spring when I'm out. Freedom! And I'll be able to bring Ethan back to see you guys.

Lots of love
Jack (or Justin because I know it weirds you out calling me Jack, haha!) xx

Jack was right, of course. Our house had been suitably festooned, complete with my usual three Christmas trees, since the end of November. And, oh the joy of our fancy new open-plan space; I'd never had such a huge room to decorate before, or space for such a ridiculously large tree. But I wasn't just jumping the gun. We had wanted to do something especially for Ethan (as if I needed an excuse!) before he left us to go live with his grandparents, including a little pre-Christmas farewell party. It had taken precisely two months from start to finish for the court orders to be signed off and for Jocelyn and Alan to be prepared to have Ethan move in fully with them, so after two overnight stays to help with the transition, they came to collect him finally on 2 December.

As emotional farewells go, Ethan's was a weird one. I'm normally all braced for the floodgates to open, but when we saw Ethan off it felt more like we'd had one of the grandchildren to stay for a week, and now they were heading back to Mum and Dad. At the time, I didn't understand why I felt the way I did – was I getting tougher in my old age, or what? Or was it simply that Ethan had been with us for so short a time, and that, knowing his future lay with his own grandparents and father, I had none of the usual anxieties about things working out with a new foster or adoptive family?

On reflection, though, I think it was down to Jack. This was Jack's boy, which meant he felt a part of the family automatically now, but it was more than that; the connection had had one other unexpected consequence – the friendly relationship I'd built with Jocelyn Baines, and that sense, going forward, that the contact would continue for as long as she might need it, as she navigated her unexpected new role.

I Want My Daddy

There was one huge reason for moving on happily and swiftly, however; as Jack had said, the much anticipated 'Wedding of the Year'. (Or was it Wedding of the Century? Almost certainly.) It also fell on my dad's birthday, which was just a few days before Christmas, and, despite my ending up having very little do with it, the whole thing went off like a dream. And even though I say so myself, my mother of the groom outfit was absolutely bloody gorgeous and I felt like the *grand dame* of the ball. Mind you, that feeling didn't last for very long. By Christmas Day, when I was indeed running around like a blue-arsed fly in the kitchen plating up sixteen Christmas dinners, I wasn't so much *grand dame* as an elderly Cinderella; though regular readers know I wouldn't have it any other way.

Ethan settled in beautifully with his doting grandparents, and with home feeling secure for him, he blossomed equally quickly at his new school. Given his special needs, he was allocated a permanent one-to-one assistant, and was thriving to an extent that the various labels that had been attached to him were soon scheduled for professional review. He never did need to get allocated that child psychologist, either. It was agreed it wasn't needed.

To my delight, Ethan also liked to keep in touch – something I didn't and don't doubt was all part of us having that shared loved one, in the shape of his father. It soon felt completely natural that I would get a FaceTime call at least once a week from him, gushing about his new friends or what he'd been up to with Grannie and Pops.

Jocelyn would phone me regularly as well, just as I'd encouraged her to do. Not so I could try and influence her where Jack was concerned, but simply to support her wherever I could, as I was mindful that most of the school mums she'd encounter would be thirty-odd years younger than she was, and it was good to have another mum to bounce off. She'd wait till Ethan was in bed, but sometimes it wasn't even about him. She'd ring to tell me about a fabulous book she'd read, or a new series on TV she thought I might like. Sometimes she phoned just to chat about Brogan. I got the feeling it mattered greatly to her that I got a fuller sense of the daughter she loved, and didn't just see her as a 'bad' mother. Which, of course, I didn't. My hatred was always, always for the drugs. But again, our chats felt like the most natural thing in the world.

As for Jack, I just know that he's going to do well too. He's out of prison now, of course, and is working very hard, saving up for that little home he's always wanted. He sees Ethan all the time – as I write, every weekend – and has even been allowed to take him away for two nights, to a holiday park near to where he now lives. But the best thing of all is that Jocelyn and Alan are so impressed with how Jack has been doing that, given their ages, they have already made a sensible and pragmatic decision. They've suggested that in a couple of years, if all goes to plan, they will help him get joint custody of Ethan and will even help him out with the deposit to buy that all-important home.

So though Ethan gave me and Mike a wake-up call regarding our ages (and how!) he really did have the happiest of endings.

CASEY WATSON

---

*One woman determined to
make a difference.*

*Read Casey's poignant
memoirs and be inspired.*

I JUST WANT TO BE LOVED

Casey has fostered her share of vulnerable adolescents, but 14-year-old Elise brings her own unique challenges

When Elise makes some dark allegations against her mum, who has recently come back into her life, Casey doesn't know what to believe. Is Elise telling the truth? Casey is determined to find out and keep her safe.

MUMMY, PLEASE DON'T LEAVE

When baby Tommy – born in prison – and his half-brother, Seth, are placed in the Watsons' care, their troubled teenage mother soon follows suit

Can Casey find the energy and strength to see this unusual case through?

LET ME GO

Harley is an anxious teen
who wants to end her own life,
and there's only one woman
who can find out why

Casey makes a breakthrough which
sheds light on the disturbing truth –
there is a man in Harley's life, a
very dangerous man indeed.

A DARK SECRET

A troubled nine-year-old with
a violent streak, Sam's relentless
bullying sees even his siblings beg
not to be placed with him

When Casey delves into Sam's past
she uncovers something far darker
than she had imagined.

A BOY WITHOUT HOPE

A history of abuse and neglect
has left Miller destined for
life's scrap heap

Miller's destructive behaviour will push
Casey to her limits, but she is determined
to help him overcome his demons
and give him hope.

NOWHERE TO GO

Eleven-year-old Tyler has stabbed his stepmother and has nowhere to go

With his birth mother dead and a father who doesn't want him, what can be done to stop his young life spiralling out of control?

GROOMED

Keeley is urgently rehomed with Casey after accusing her foster father of abuse

It's Casey's job to keep Keeley safe, but can she protect this strong-willed teen from the dangers online?

THE SILENT WITNESS

Bella's father is on a ventilator, fighting for his life, while her mother is currently on remand in prison, charged with his attempted murder

Bella is the only witness.

RUNAWAY GIRL

Adrianna arrives on Casey's doorstep with no possessions, no English and no explanation

It will be a few weeks before Casey starts getting the shocking answers to her questions . . .

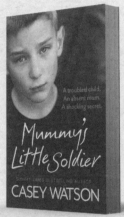

MUMMY'S LITTLE SOLDIER

Leo isn't a bad lad, but his frequent absences from school mean he's on the brink of permanent exclusion

Leo is clearly hiding something, and Casey knows that if he is to have any kind of future, it's up to her to find out the truth.

SKIN DEEP

Flip is being raised by her alcoholic mother, and comes to Casey after a fire at their home

Flip has Foetal Alcohol Syndrome (FAS), but it soon turns out that this is just the tip of the iceberg . . .

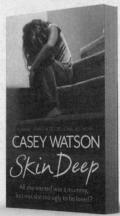

A STOLEN CHILDHOOD

Kiara appears tired and distressed, and the school wants Casey to take her under her wing for a while

On the surface, everything points to a child who is upset that her parents have separated. The horrific truth, however, shocks Casey to the core.

THE GIRL WITHOUT A VOICE

What is the secret behind Imogen's silence?

Discover the shocking and devastating past of a child with severe behavioural problems.

A LAST KISS FOR MUMMY

A teenage mother and baby in need of a loving home

At fourteen, Emma is just a child herself – and one who's never been properly mothered.

BREAKING THE SILENCE

Two boys with an unlikely bond

With Georgie and Jenson, Casey is facing her toughest test yet.

MUMMY'S LITTLE HELPER

A young girl secretly caring for her mother

Abigail has been dealing with pressures no child should face. Casey has the difficult challenge of helping her to learn to let go.

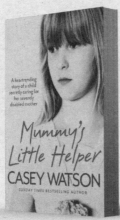

TOO HURT TO STAY

Branded 'vicious and evil', eight-year-old Spencer asks to be taken into care

Casey and her family are disgusted: kids aren't born evil. Despite the challenges Spencer brings, they are determined to help him find a loving home.

LITTLE PRISONERS

Abused siblings who do not know what it means to be loved

With new-found security and trust, Casey helps Ashton and Olivia to rebuild their lives

CRYING FOR HELP

A damaged girl haunted by her past

Sophia pushes Casey to the limits, threatening the safety of the whole family. Can Casey make a difference in time?

THE BOY NO ONE LOVED

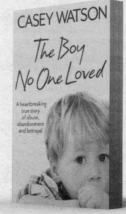

Five-year-old Justin was desperate and helpless

Six years after being taken into care, Justin has had 20 failed placements. Casey and her family are his last hope.

TITLES AVAILABLE AS E-BOOK ONLY

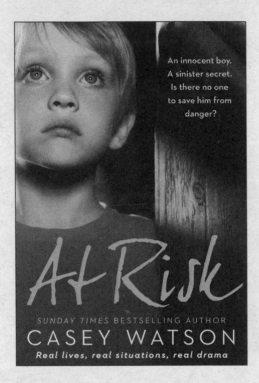

AT RISK

Adam is brought to Casey while his mum recovers in hospital – just for a few days

But a chance discovery reveals that Casey has stumbled upon something altogether more sinister . . .

THE LITTLE PRINCESS

Six-year-old Darby is naturally distressed at being removed from her parents just before Christmas

And when the shocking and sickening reason is revealed, a Happy New Year seems an impossible dream as well . . .

DADDY'S BOY

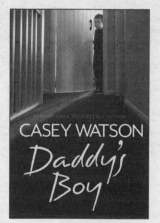

Paulie, just five, is a boy out of control – or is he just misunderstood?

The plan for Paulie is simple: get him back home with his family. But perhaps 'home' isn't the best place for him . . .

THE WILD CHILD

Angry and hurting, eight-year-old Connor is from a broken home

As streetwise as they come, he's determined to cause trouble. But Casey is convinced there is a frightened child beneath the swagger.

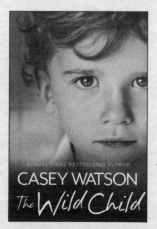

NO PLACE FOR NATHAN

Nathan has a sometime alter ego called Jenny who is the only one who knows the secrets of his disturbed past

But where is Jenny when she is most needed?

SCARLETT'S SECRET

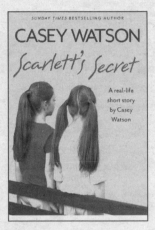

Jade and Scarlett, seventeen-year-old twins, share a terrible secret

Can Casey help them come to terms with the truth and rediscover their sibling connection?

JUST A BOY

Cameron is a sweet boy who seems happy in his skin – making him rather different from most of the other children Casey has cared for

But what happens when Cameron disappears? Will Casey's worst fears be realised?

FEEL HEART.
FEEL HOPE.
READ CASEY.

Discover more about Casey Watson.
Visit www.caseywatson.co.uk

Find Casey Watson on **f** & 🐦

MOVING
Memoirs

Stories of hope, courage and
the power of love . . .

Sign up to the Moving Memoirs email and you'll
be the first to hear about new books, discounts,
and get sneak previews from your
favourite authors!

Sign up at

www.moving-memoirs.com